The Gospel of John,
One Day at a Time

*A Seven-Week Guide
for New – and
not-so-new – Believers*

Timothy C. McKeown

outskirts
press

Dedication

*I dedicate this book to the pastors with whom I have
served and from whom I have learned so much:*

To Dr. Joe Griffith, the pastor who taught me how to join hearts;

To Rev. Ray Rogers, who encouraged my first steps in ministry;

*To Dr. D.L. Lowrie, who as my pastor at First Baptist Church of Lubbock
inspired me each week as a college student and endorsed me to attend seminary;*

To Rev. Bob Cameron, who believed in me with my first ministry;

*To Dr. J. Tom Shelton, who preached my ordination service and
continues to be an inspiration in Christian faithfulness;*

To Dr. Kenny Lewis, who first walked me through life-long disciple-making;

*To Dr. Gordon Malkowski, now with the Lord, who
showed how to bravely face physical death;*

To Rev. Dale Perry, who taught me about true forgiveness;

*To Dr. Randall Wallace, who more than any other has truly
been a pastor and friend to me when I needed it most.*

Table of Contents

Preface

Over the last twenty years or so, I have examined, written, and rewritten these daily devotionals on John's gospel. The word of God never grows old. I have self-published elements of this study, emailed it out, published it on my blog (see john-oneday.blogspot.com), and now printed it in this book form.

My love for the gospel is not at all unique. Frequently, people will tell new believers to read the Gospel of John, although without a good study companion for the new believer, the Gospel of Mark might be a little easier to read and understand. The depth and significance of the fourth gospel is why I wrote this study. When I began these writings, I could not find a "Gospel of John for Dummies." Even now, despite the high number of devotionals and commentaries, I still am hard-pressed to find a "basics for believers" explanation of this gospel. Because of all of this, I am publishing this book of devotionals.

Several years ago, a word-for-word dramatization of the Gospel of John was released to theaters and then to DVD, using the Good News Translation, narrated by Christopher Plummer (Captain von Trapp in *The Sound of Music*). While I do not endorse the critical commentaries that accompany that video, for the sake of new believers, I greatly appreciate the easy-to-understand translation chosen.

You see, the Gospel of John is the deepest of all of the gospels and perhaps the most contemplative of all of the books in the New Testament. This devotional book is designed for new believers and young disciples to dig deeply into the most reflective of the four gospels. Where Matthew, Mark, and Luke tell more of what Jesus *did*, the primary concern of John, "the disciple whom Jesus loved," is to tell what Jesus *taught*—and why. The Beloved Apostle himself wrote that he included only a few of the signs which Jesus performed for a purpose: *"But these are written that you may believe that Jesus is the Christ, the Son of God, and that believing you may have life in His name"* (John 20:31, NKJV).

From the beginning, my desire was for new believers to study this amazing story of Christ on a daily basis, but in small "bite-sized" devotionals of 500 words or less. I have also put some things in this devotional that I hope will inspire the more mature Christian. I invite you to join with me for the next fifty days, morning and evening, to see how God calls us to truly live in Him. My goal is to help new believers grow and for the more seasoned believers to grow deeper from this rich and enlightening gospel. The book of John, like the rest of the Bible, is as interesting as the ocean's depths, where scientists may never cease to explore but also as inviting as the coastal shore, where even the youngest of children may play.

John said his purpose in writing was that the reader would believe in Jesus Christ; that is, place one's trust for eternal life in the finished work of His sacrificial death and that the reader would also have life in His name. John would later write, *"These things I have written to you who believe in the name of the Son of God, that* *you may <u>know</u> that you have eternal life, and that you may continue to believe in the name of the Son of God."* (1 John 5:13, NKJV, emphasis mine) God wants everyone to believe in Him and to have eternal life, so He made it as easy as "A B C".

"A" Admit your imperfections: First of all, the Bible says we must "A" Admit that we are not perfect and are not good enough to go to heaven. Romans 3:23 says that we have all sinned and have all come short of His glorious perfection. Admitting that we are going in the wrong direction is the first step to turning around to go in the right direction. That is what the word "repent" means, and it was the first message Jesus proclaimed (Mark 1:15). Will you admit that you have sinned, that you are not perfect, and that you need to turn to God?

"B" Believe in Christ: Second, the Bible teaches we must "B" Believe or put our faith and trust in Jesus Christ. John 3:16 says whoever believes in God's Son will not perish but will have eternal life. Belief is not just head knowledge but a "heart-trusting" faith that when Jesus died on the cross, He paid sin's penalty of death. True saving faith can be illustrated in a person who is trying to swim from Los Angeles to Hawaii. When that person sees a ship going by, he can believe in his head that the ship exists but if he continues to put his trust in his own swimming to get himself to Hawaii, he will never make it. Like the swimmer, you must admit you cannot make it on your own and put your trust in the "ship" named Jesus Christ so that you actually get onboard to make it to your destination.

"C" Call on the name of the Lord Jesus Christ: Third, the Bible proclaims you must "C" Call upon the name of the Lord. Romans 10:13 says quite simply that whoever calls on the name of the Lord shall be saved. Saved from what? We are saved from eternal death and separation from God. The Bible says that without faith, unbelievers will suffer from eternal destruction and being *"away from the presence of the Lord"* (2 Thessalonians 1:9, ESV).

Like a man awaiting a response to his proposal of marriage, Christ wants you to respond with a YES to His invitation. Do not leave this "proposal" hanging. The Bible warns if you hear His voice today, do not harden your heart. (See Hebrews 4:7 and 2 Corinthians 6:2.)

The Bible calls your new life in Christ many things: salvation, redemption, having eternal life, and these are just a few. John quotes Jesus as calling salvation being "born again" (see John 3:3, 7), and Peter had written earlier, *"For you have been born again, not of perishable seed, but of imperishable, through the living and enduring word of God."* (1 Peter 1:23, NIV) Being born physically is not the end but rather the beginning. In the same way, being spiritually born again is just the beginning of your spiritual and eternal life. In other words, this changes everything.

If you have not placed your trust and faith in Christ alone for your salvation, or if you are not sure you have eternal life, do what the Apostle John desired his readers to do. Simply but sincerely place your faith and trust in Christ as the Son of God and receive life in His name. Pray to God a simple prayer like this: *"Dear God, I admit that I'm a sinner, and I know that I am not perfect. I believe Jesus died on the cross to take away my sins, and I believe You raised Him from the dead to give me* eternal life. I call in faith for You to come into my life. I confess You as my Savior and my Lord, and I commit my life to You. In Jesus's Name, Amen."

If you have trusted Jesus Christ as your Lord and Savior, you may ask, "Now what?" Well, now you grow. A newborn yearns for nourishment, but a mother's milk is only the start. Here is another "A B C" for believers:

"A" Assurance: Jesus said in John 6:47, *"Most assuredly I say to you, he who believes in Me has eternal life."* No one can snatch you from the Father's hand (John 10:28–29), not even you or your sins of the past, present, or future! Our assurance of having eternal life does not depend on how good we are but how good God is. In Hebrews 13:5, God promises us that He will never leave us nor forsake us; therefore, we do not have to be afraid of losing our salvation. If we were saved by our faith but kept saved by our good works, that simply would not make sense. If none of us are good enough to be saved by our works in the first place, then none of us would be good enough to be kept saved by our works. Eternal life that only lasts for a day, a week, a month, even for years, but then can be lost is simply not, by definition, eternal life. Rest assured that just as Paul said in Philippians 1:6, *"I am sure of this, that He who began a good work in you will bring it to completion at the day of Jesus Christ."*

"B" Baptism: John the Baptist baptized Jesus, so we should follow the Lord's example and be baptized. Being fully immersed in water symbolizes being cleansed from sin (Acts 22:16), being raised to walk in new life (Romans 6:4), and being immersed in the Holy Spirit (John 1:33).

"C" Church membership: The Bible says the church is Christ's body (Ephesians 5:23; Colossians 1:18), and we are members of one another (Ephesians 4:25; Romans 12:5). When we are born physically, we are part of both the human race and also a local family. When we are born again spiritually, we are members of both the universal church and should also be a part of a local family of believers.

There is even a "D" for Discipleship: We are created in Christ Jesus for good works (Ephesians 2:8–10). By having assurance of our salvation and being baptized into a local church body, we are now ready to grow deeper as a disciple.

Are you ready? Let us walk together, one day at a time, and learn the depths of what Christ defines as eternal life in John 17:3 where He said, *"And this is eternal life, that they know You, the only true God, and Jesus Christ whom you have sent"* (NKJV).

Finally, because there are so many different translations of the Bible, new believers sometimes wonder "which version is the best." I believe the best version is whichever one that encourages you to keep on reading, so if the Bible you are reading is too hard to understand, find an easier translation.

The movie *The Gospel of John* uses the Good News Translation (GNT) or sometimes called Today's English Version (TEV). That was one of the first easy-to-read translations in English (although some think it goes *too* far away in its simplification from the Greek language, which was the original language of the New Testament). The hardest English translation to understand is perhaps the King James Version, and yet so many people have often heard the Bible quoted in that 400-year-old translation, which uses ancient words like "thee" and "thou."

I sometimes will ask you to look up a verse and fill in the blank, so I am primarily going to use the New King James Version (NKJV), which is somewhere in between the Good News Translation and the King James Version. Unless otherwise indicated, all verses quoted will be NKJV. There are a number of internet sites that you can visit and look up other translations to help you understand a passage a little more easily. I will also use other translations, including the New International Version (NIV), the English Standard Version (ESV), and the Christian Standard Bible (CSB).

May this devotional book be as much of a blessing to you to read as it was for me to write.

Timothy C. McKeown
February 13, 2019

The Gospel of John

Author: John the apostle, son of Zebedee and brother of fellow apostle, James, who was the first apostle to die. John was the last of the original 12 disciples to face death.

Date: AD 80–90

Location of writing: Church of Ephesus

To whom was it written: Jews and Gentiles

Purpose: To show Jesus as Christ who gives eternal life

—John Chapter 1—

Memory Verse:

In the beginning was the Word, and the Word
was with God, and the Word was God...
And the Word became flesh and dwelt among us.

(John 1:1, 14a)

(NOTE: Several of the chapters will have fictional, imaginative vignettes)

The old man drummed his stubbly, once-calloused fingers on the small wooden table, pondering his years of loyal but sometimes anguished service to His Lord and Master. He surely felt his age, and he could deny no longer the ebbing of time to tell his story about his walk with the Lamb of God. But where to begin?

The old fisherman bellowed a laughed so loud that he startled his loyal scribe. *"Beh-Ray-SHEETH!"* He bellowed even louder than his laugh.

"What did you say?" said the young companion.

"Come now," the pastor winked at the youth helping him with pen and parchment as well as smoothing out his horrible Greek. "Your Hebrew can't be that rusty."

"Aramaic, yes," the lad protested sincerely. "But Hebrew? Say it again, without that Galilean twang."

"B'reshiyth! In the beginning..." His crackling voice graveled slowly out. The scribe quickly saw his mentor was not dictating a new letter to a distant church. He was not rewriting the first book of the Torah. The elder did not continue with "... *God created the heavens and the earth"* but with *"...was the Word."* At last, he was finally transcribing the first words of the long-awaited gospel from the sole remaining eyewitness of the Messiah.

Unmistakably Jewish, the aged apostle was keenly aware of the growing Greek influence on the church. The elect body was being formed from all nations, fulfilling the prophecy that the Christ would indeed be *"a Light to the Gentiles".*

This gospel would be focused on "the Word". *Logos*, yes, *LOGOS*, the pregnant Greek word was richly nuanced with so many subtle meanings. The old man wanted all glory and all focus to be on the Light, the Life, the Lamb, the *Logos*.

But in the beginning of the beginning would be a witness of the Word.

And the witness's name was John!

Day 1: Morning
Salvation: Receive The Light
(Read John 1:1–14)

I was a child when I received Jesus Christ into my life. Like today's title says, it was like receiving a light into my life and ever since then, I have tried to shine that light to others. Salvation is like receiving the light. We previously were in spiritual darkness. Think about some characteristics given of "the Word."

Verse 1--the Word was *"in the beginning,"* the *"Word was with God,"* and *"the Word was God."*

"In the beginning was the Word" is reminiscent of Genesis 1:1 *"In the beginning, God created the heavens and the earth."* This passage tells us that "the Word" (in the Greek: *logos*) is Jesus Christ; Jesus has always existed; and Jesus is God. Yet He became a human being and can identify with us.

> In the next seven weeks you will learn these Basics for New Believers

GROWTH
God At the Center of Life
Read The Word Daily
Obedience To Christ
Witness to Others
Talk with God in Prayer
Healthy Church Fellowship

OTHER LESSONS
Assurance of salvation
Baptism's Meaning
Communion's Meaning
Deeper Discipleship

When you hear the word "dog," an image of a barking four-legged animal with a tail comes to mind. A single word can represent a person, place or thing. Jesus Christ is "the Word" and He represents the infinite God to a finite world. Jesus was the physical manifestation of the heavenly Father and revealed the unseen God (see verse 18).

Verse 13 means that you do not have to be a certain race (blood) to become a child of God. Your <u>physical</u> birth was a result of the will of your parents, but your <u>spiritual</u> birth is a result of the will of God.

There is a funny story about a teenager who, frustrated with her parents, shouted, "Hey, I never asked to be born!" Equally frustrated, the mother replied, "That's good, because if you had, I would have said 'No!'"

In a way, God wants you to "ask to be born" by receiving and believing in His name.

Pray this prayer to God: *"Heavenly Father: Thank You for letting me become Your child and for giving me light to walk in this life. Help me to be a reflection of Your light to this world by letting Jesus shine through me. Amen."*

DAY 1: EVENING
What Baptism Means
(Read John 1:15–34)

When I was baptized, I told a friend at school that it was "neater than going swimming." And it really was. John the Baptist's baptisms were for repentance or a turning away from sins. He also spoke of someone who was greater than he who would not only help us turn from our sins but would also forgive us of all of our sins. Look up Acts 19:1–5 where some of John's disciples would later be baptized again in the name of Jesus.

John the Baptist preached that someone special was about to come, even though he did not know that Jesus was the Messiah (verse 31). John "bore witness" of a coming Christ or Messiah (see 1:15, 19, and 32).

To *witness* means to tell others what you have seen. As a Christian, you have a wonderful opportunity to share about your new life in Christ with others. One way you can witness is to be baptized.

Jesus said we are to be baptized in the name of the Father, Son, and Holy Spirit (Matthew 28:19). Baptism symbolizes <u>God the Father</u> washing away our sins (see Acts 22:16). It pictures our identification with the death, burial, and resurrection of <u>the Son</u> (see Romans 6:4) and it represents the immersion of <u>the Holy Spirit</u> into our lives (see John 1:34 and Acts 1:5). In other words, the Holy Spirit of God, the same Spirit Who was in Jesus, gets all of us, and we get all of Him.

Do not wait to be water baptized. Acts 22:16 says, *"Why are you waiting? Arise and be baptized. Wash away your sins by calling on the name of the Lord"* (author's paraphrase). In Matthew 3:13–17, Jesus said that His baptism was the right thing to do. When you are baptized, you are following His example.

There is a fifth reason to be baptized: Jesus commanded us to do so (Matthew 28:19–20). We want to do as He did and obey what He commanded us to do.

Over the years, I have learned baptism is more than just being "neater than going swimming." It shows God has washed away my sins. It shows that I have a new life in Christ, and baptism symbolizes that God's Spirit is now to saturate my life. Baptism follows His example and command.

Pray this prayer to God: *"Dear God, help me be a witness for You and tell others what You have done in my life. Help me not just talk the talk, but also walk the walk as a believer in Jesus Christ. Amen."*

DAY 2: MORNING
Quiet Times: Spending Time With Jesus
(Read John 1:35–51)

Early in a new believer's life, the Christian needs to seek out Jesus and spend time with Him. In John 1:37–39, Andrew and another disciple wanted to spend time with Jesus. They wanted to know where He lived.

A daily time alone with God is called a "quiet time" and is essential for a Christian to grow in relationship with God. As a result of spending time with Jesus, Andrew told Simon (v. 41) and Philip told Nathanael (v. 45).

We are not given his name, but the "other disciple" was John the apostle, the author of this gospel. These five disciples (Andrew, Simon Peter, Phillip, Nathanael, and John) did not know everything, but what they knew, they shared. Their simple message: "We found Him!"

> ### Acts 1:8
>
> A witness is someone who gives a testimony about something they have seen, heard, or have knowledge about.

Verses 47–51 tell us something even greater than about finding Jesus. Nathanael discovered that Jesus already knew him! God created us and even if you have just recently come to know God, God knew you before the creation of the world.

In John 1:51, Jesus refers to Jacob's ladder (Genesis 28:12), saying that Nathanael will see angels ascending and descending on the Son of Man. Symbolically, Jesus was saying that through Him, we have access to God. Today, God "descends" to us through ways such as reading the Bible and we can "ascend" to Him in ways such as praying. Commit to God to have a quiet time each day by signing your name below:

I commit to spend time with God.

Time: _____Place: _____

Your signature:_____

Jesus invited John and Andrew to "come and see" where He lived. In order to follow Christ, we must spend time with Him. Come and see what Christ has for you each morning and night for the next seven weeks.

Pray this prayer to God: *"Father, help me to have a daily quiet time with You. Give me a desire to see where you live. Thank You that before I found You, You saw me and loved me. I am so glad I found You! Amen."*

DAY 2: EVENING
Seven Sevens of Lessons
(John 1:35–51)

Seven is a holy number for Jews, a sign of perfection and completion. In chapter 1, we see the first of seven "witnesses" or "testimonies" of Jesus being the Christ, the Anointed Messiah, promised in the Old Testament to come.

The Greek word for witness or testimony is *martyr*. In English, "martyrs" are those who make a testimony and sacrifice their own lives for their beliefs. The seven witnesses John records are

1) Witness of John the Baptist (John 1:7–8; 5:33–36);
2) Witness of works (John 5:36);
3) Witness of the Father (John 5:37, 8:18);
4) Witness of the Scriptures (John 5:39, 45–47);
5) Witness of Himself (John 5:31; 8:14–18);
6) Witness of the disciples (John 12:17; 15:27; 19:35; 21:24); and
7) Witness of the Holy Spirit (John 15:26).

In total, there are seven lessons with seven sub-points in John. In addition to the

1. Seven witnesses (testimonies) for Christ; we will see
2. Seven "Transitive I AM" statements (we will discuss this on Day 11);
3. Seven "Intransitive I AM" statements in which Jesus said "I AM" with no direct object (see Day 7);
4. Seven miraculous signs (see Day 11);
5. Seven comparisons to God the Father, ("as the Father...so do I", see Day 9);
6. Seven journeys to Jerusalem, (found in John chapters 1, 3, 5, 7, 8, 11, and 12);
7. Seven major sermons:
   (1). New Birth, John 3:1–21; **(2).** Water of Life, John 4:1–42; **(3).** Equality with the Father, John 5:19–47; **(4).** Bread of Life, John 6:22–66; **(5).** Life-giving Spirit, John 7:1–52; **(6).** Light of the World (John 8:12–59); and **(7).** The Shepherd (John 10:1–21).

So, what does this mean? These repetitions of seven are "witnesses" and "testimonies" of the completion of this gospel. John, the "beloved disciple," was an eyewitness of these events and had decades to write this beautiful gospel.

Pray this prayer to God: *"Lord, as I finish this first chapter, quicken my heart in the mornings and focus my attention at night to learn from Your Spirit. Help me apply these truths from John's writings to my life. In the name of Jesus, I pray. Amen."*

TRANSITIVE "I AM"	MIRACLE SIGN	SPIRITUAL SIGNIFICANCE
Bread of Life (John 6:35–51)	Feeding of 5,000	Jesus Is Spiritual Life
Light of World (John 8:12)	Healing the Blind Man	Jesus Is Glory of God
Door of Sheep (John 10:2-9)	Healing the Lame Man	Jesus Is Freedom from Sin
Good Shepherd (John 10:11-14)	Jesus Walking On Water (John 6:16-21)	Jesus Is Our Protector
Resurrection And the Life (John 11:25)	Raising of Lazarus (John 11:1-44)	Jesus Is Eternal Life
Way, the Truth And the Life (John 14:6)	Healing the Nobleman's Son (John 4:46)	Jesus Is Our Savior
True Vine (John 15:1-5)	Turning Water Into Wine (John 2:1-11)	Jesus Is Supplier of the Fruit of the Spirit

This chart shows the "I AM" Statements with direct objects and their meanings and related miracles.

—John Chapter 2—

MEMORY VERSE:
This beginning of signs Jesus did in Cana of Galilee, and manifested His glory; and His disciples believed in Him.

(John 2:11)

Over the years, the Lord's mother had answered nearly every question the young pastor could ask her. Mary and her "adopted son" had cared for each other following the Resurrection, but the aged apostle not only survived the other disciples, but even outlived his own mother's sister. The widowed mother of Christ was only a few years older than the youngest of disciples. And perhaps because of her Son's great love for her and fond affection for the youngest of Zebedee's boys, Jesus had entrusted the care for his mother to the beloved disciple. And since the Lord knew all things, Christ also likely knew that John's life would be the longest.

John decided he would tell about the time when in Cana one of Mary's friends was so impoverished that they could not afford enough wine to serve the many guests who had come to the wedding. Jesus, a young prophet, had gathered such a following that His entourage of disciples as well as his brothers and sisters likely added to the problem of an overabundance of wine bibbers and an under abundance of wine to bib. So, what was the mother of Christ to do? She called in a favor from her firstborn Son.

The Evangelist licked his lips as if by doing so it could bring back the heavenly taste of a beverage that, quite literally, was out of this world. Wine from water pots meant to purify? What was the meaning of this, the first of all miracles? He, in typical form of his parable-loving Rabbi, would leave that mystery up to the readers of his gospel.

He smiled as he poured the fruit of the vine into his cup and gave thanks. The elder also thought not only of the first, but also the last drink he had with his Master. How he longed for that future supper in heaven. "I cannot wait to taste that wine again," he said, toasting his goblet skyward with a whimsical upward look to his unseen home.

His mouth quickly turned downward as if he had suddenly tasted a bitter wormwood scroll. He sullenly slammed the goblet down to the table a little harder than he intended. Looking at his current beverage and comparing it to his long distant memory of the succulence of that miraculous wine, he mused, "Not even close!"

DAY 3: MORNING
Submission: Go To God With Everything
(Read John 2:1–5)

When was the first time you really felt like "an adult"? Was it buying a car, getting a job, getting married or even having a baby? How do you feel when you go back home to your parents? Today, we see Jesus in His home environment, Nazareth, and with His mother.

Sometimes we forget that Jesus was a real human who ate, drank, got sleepy, and even went to parties such as this wedding. It is, to say the least, interesting to see Jesus, at 30 years of age, interacting with His mother. She knew her Son better than anyone else. She knew for certain He was divinely conceived (Luke 1:35). And she knew she could go to Jesus with a problem of running out of wine.

There is nothing too big for God to handle, but there is also nothing too small. You may be tempted to say, "God, I'll call on you if there is something too big I can't handle." But the Bible says for us to go to God in everything. *"Don't worry about anything, but in everything, through prayer and petition with thanksgiving, let your requests be made known to God."* (Philippians 4:6, HCSB).

> **Matthew 6:33**
>
> Submission is hard because we don't want anyone, even God, telling us what to do.

Submission is difficult because we don't want anyone telling us what to do. When we go to God with everything, we are submitting everything to His care and control. The response of Jesus to his mother may at first seem harsh. Sometimes our prayers may seem like they are getting the same cool response from God. Despite her Son's response, Mary told the servants to do whatever Jesus said. When we go to God in prayer, we should fully expect Him to answer and we should be willing to do whatever He says.

If we want God to help us in the everyday problems of life, we must go to Him in everything like Mary did. We should also follow Mary's instructions: *"Whatever He says to you, do it."*

Pray this prayer to God: *"Our Father in Heaven. I come today with my daily needs, my dreams, and my wishes. Thank You that I can pray about everything big or small. In Your Name I pray. Amen."*

Day 3: Evening
When Water Turns Into Wine: The Best Is Yet To Come
(Read John 2:1–11)

The Lord's glory was revealed in this miracle and led the disciples to believe in Him (2:11). This miracle had several purposes.

1) The water pots were used for religious purification. Turning the water into wine showed Christ's superiority over ritual (2:6). Elsewhere, wine symbolizes Christ's blood (Matthew 26:28; Mark 14:24; Luke 22:20; and 1 Corinthians 10:16). When we partake of Communion ("the Lord's Supper"), we remember Christ's sacrifice. We contemplate our "common union" with Christ and our fellow Christians. We are encouraged to look forward to Christ's coming again (1 Corinthians 10:16–17, 11:25–28; Matthew 26:29)

2) The master of the feast said the world offers its best first and later brings out the lesser. With Christianity, suffering occurs in this world, but in the next world, the best is yet to come. One preacher said, "Let us pour away all the vinegar of this world, for the best wine is coming."

3) The master of the wedding also did not know from where the wine came. The thought in those days was that no one would know from where the Christ would come. The wine's secret origin is like Jesus being hidden from the world but part of God's plan from the beginning. Besides the wine, there are other references about not knowing where Christ comes from:

The Wind: *"you do not know where it comes from"* (3:8)

The Water: *"from where will you get the living water?"* (4:11)

The Where: *"when Christ comes, no one knows where He is from."* (7:27)

The Witness: *"My witness is true for I know where I came from…but you do not know where I come from."* (8:14)

The Worshiper: *"…as for this Fellow, we do not know where He is from…this is a marvelous thing that you do not know where He is from…If anyone is a worshiper of God…He hears him"* (9:29–33)

The Wonder: *"Where are You from?" But Jesus gave him no answer.* (19:9)

Pray this prayer to God: *"Thank You Jesus that You are greater than religion. Thank you that the best is yet to come. Help me to show others where You came from so that they can know where they can go. Amen."*

DAY 4: MORNING
What Does The First Miracle Affirm?
(Read John 2:1–11)

In the Greek language (the language the New Testament was originally written in), there are no separate words for "grape juice" and "wine." In other words, wine did not always mean an alcoholic drink.

The head master said the wine was superior to anything he had tasted. One Biblical scholar, Albert Barnes, cites three ancient Greek sources which said that "good wine" in those days meant *not* fermented. Jesus also made it in abundance, as much as 135 gallons. By creating so much, and making it so succulent, those who drank it likely drank plenty of it!

Ephesians 5:18 says, *"Don't get drunk with wine, which leads to reckless actions, but be filled with the Spirit"* (HCSB). Since it is wrong to get drunk, it is hard to imagine Jesus making so much of the beverage and making it fermented (especially when it tasted so good) and still expect people not to get drunk by it.

This was the first of seven miraculous signs which John recorded. Other lessons from this include the following:

Christ affirms marriage: Jesus performed His first miracle at a wedding. God's first commandment in Genesis 2 implies marriage. The joining of a man and a woman in marriage is seen as the last symbolic image of Christ and the church in Revelation. Christ affirms marriage.

Christ affirms motherhood: Jesus solved His mother's problem as a dutiful Son, just as He was to His Heavenly Father (see Luke 2:51). It was not rude to call His mother woman, as He even did so at the tender moment of His death (John 19:26).

Christ affirms merriment: Jesus was invited to this wedding and did not shun joyful gatherings. Wine was given by God to give joy (Psalm 104:15; Ecclesiastes 9:7) and the miracle affirms our abundant life (John 10:10).

Christ affirms the miraculous: Jesus's first miracle revealed God's glory (2:11) and gave a basis for the faith in His disciples.

Pray this prayer to God: *"Thank You Jesus for joy, for families and companionships with other believers, and for affirming marriages and family relationships. In Your holy name I pray. Amen."*

DAY 4: EVENING
What Is Your Motivation?
(Read John 2:12–25)

The cleansing of the Temple actually occurs twice, and both times it occurs around the time of Passover. Here, it is at the beginning of His ministry, but the other gospels record a second cleansing just prior to Jesus's crucifixion.

Jesus saw people using God and His temple for their own profit and showed what we call "righteous indignation." Being angry for the right things is not a sin!

John's gospel was the last to be written. Yet he leaves out many of the other miracles which Jesus performed. This is the opposite of legends and folklore, which tend to exaggerate as time goes on. John however wrote more about the *teachings* of Jesus rather than the *miracles* of Jesus.

Jesus did not entrust Himself (or "commit" Himself, NKJV) to those who followed Him of His miracles--He knew what was in their hearts (2:24–25). But our true motive of our faith in Christ should be the resurrection (see John 2:19–22)

Examine your motives for following Christ. Are you following Him because of His miracles or His message (eternal life and victory over sin)?

If Jesus did not commit Himself (make Himself vulnerable by putting blind trust in) the people, we should not just blindly trust people even if they call themselves believers. Just as in this lesson, the world and sadly even some in the church have less than

Mt 21:12, Mk 11:15, Lk 19:45

Compare the first "cleansing of the Temple" found in John 2 to the other, second cleansing in Matthew, Mark, and Luke. Note the similarities and differences.

pure motives. The Apostle John later wrote, *"Beloved, do not believe every spirit, but test the spirits, whether they are of God; because many false prophets have gone out into the world"* (1 John 4:1). All believers need to be in a church but never to blindly follow fallible leaders. It must be a Bible-teaching church with Bible-believing members and leaders.

Pray this prayer to God: *"Dear God, You know my heart. Test me today to see if I am serving You with the right motives. Examine my words and works, even if they may appear outwardly religious and good. Use your Holy Spirit to help me inspect the things I watch, listen to, read, and test even the spiritual leaders around me. If anything is not of You, help me to discern what is right and wrong. Amen."*

—John Chapter 3—

MEMORY VERSE:
*"For God so loved the world that He gave His only
begotten Son, that whoever believes in Him
should not perish but have everlasting life."*

(John 3:16)

"I thought he was so old then," the elder mused as he recalled first meeting the aged Pharisee, once so esteemed as were all of the religious leaders to the young fisherman. "And yet, he was younger than I am now." Nicodemus, "ruler of the people" as his name meant, was as much of a contradiction as was his name. He was hardly a ruler as the young disciple would soon learn. The old religious man didn't know as much about God as did the Teacher, even though Jesus had never been schooled in the rabbinical sense of the word.

Stories from the Law about serpents being lifted up on a staff to provide healing to those who looked up in faith was a foretaste of what Christ Himself would do. But it was not just about old men or old teachings.

The gospel was also about new beginnings, like being born again, never perishing, and having everlasting life. Jesus taught about actually knowing God and being known by Him; how a new belief would result in a new behavior; and the love, oh yes the love of God, for not just the religious or only the Jews but for all of the world.

The late meeting between Nicodemus and Jesus was as bright in the writer's memory as the light that the Lord spoke of. While Jesus's light was dawning, the young disciple's former mentor, John the Baptizer, was approaching a different twilight. His light, like his followers, was fading like a sunset on the Western Sea, and soon he would be imprisoned, silenced, and ultimately executed by Herod.

Unlike his disciples, the Baptist had no thoughts of jealousy or rivalry with his Nazarene cousin. John's life was a testimony of faith, loyalty, and love. What passion and fiery messages he brought to prepare the way of the Christ. His messages were like the two sides of the same Lake of Galilee, one choppy and full of foamy waves, and the other serene, calm, and smooth. Yet both sides shared the same waters.

The scribe broke the silent thoughts of the evangelist. "Are we finished for the night, pastor?"

"Finished?" The eyes of the pastor narrowed as they focused in on the young writer. "The night has just begun, young Tertius! Get another parchment!"

New Beginning: You Must Be Born Again
(Read John 3:1–8)

Picture this: It's very late. John, the consummate brain-picker, is alone with Jesus, asking Him more of the ministry, trying his best to understand the Messiah. Suddenly there is a knock at the door of the house. It is Nicodemus, a quiet, even mousy-type of Pharisee, who looks very out of place and uncomfortable meeting with the unorthodox Rabbi.

Jesus had come to the temple and refused to show a sign to the other Pharisees. He made a mysterious *"destroy this temple"* statement but did not explain He was speaking of the temple of His body.

> **1 Peter 1:23**
>
> Loving others sincerely is a result of being born again or "from above" through the word of God

Now read John 3:1–21 as though you were a fly on the wall with Jesus and Nicodemus. Maybe Nicodemus was afraid to be seen with Jesus so he came at night. We will see Nicodemus again later, feebly trying to defend this Man whom he believed was *"a Teacher who came from God."*

Some explain *"be born of the water"* as water baptism but that seems unlikely. As important as water baptism is, if it were *essential* to the kingdom of God, Jesus surely would have explained it better. A good way to figure out a difficult concept is to look at its context. Verse 5 is explained by verse 6. Being *"born of the water"* is physical birth; being *"born of the spirit"* is salvation or spiritual rebirth.

The word "again" literally means "from the top", and like in English, it has a literal and figurative meaning. If a musician says, "Let's take it from the top," it means "let's do this again from the beginning." Spiritual rebirth is to be born "from the top" and is the same word used in John 3:31 *"from above,"* Acts 26:5 "from the first", and Galatians 4:9 *"all over again"*. See other passages about being made new in 2 Corinthians 5:17, Titus 3:5, and 1 Peter 1:23.

Being born again is more than merely starting over. It's different than a "New Year's Resolution" that goes by the wayside in a few months. Being "born from above" means that God is now with you and in you.

Pray this prayer to God: *"Thank You Father for loving me so much that You sent Your Son to die for me. If I have never truly trusted You, I do today. Thank You that I have been born again. In the name of Jesus I pray. Amen."*

DAY 5: EVENING
New Benefit: It's Not What You Know But Whom You Know
(Read John 3:8–12)

How much do you need to understand about life in Christ in order to receive it? Do you have to understand every smallest detail in order to accept it? I do not have to understand how an airline jet works in detail in order for me to enjoy the benefits. Think of all of the things you put your faith in without knowing every answer to every question before using it.

John uses the verb "to know" frequently, usually as a deeper knowledge of God previously unknown. We don't know everything about the wind but if we put up a sail, we can enjoy the benefits of it. Fill in the blanks from the following verses (using the New King James Version).

John 3:11 — "We _____ what we <u>know</u>."

John 7:28b–29 — "He who sent Me is _____, whom you do <u>not know</u>. But I <u>know</u> Him, for I am from Him, and He sent Me."

John 8:14b —"I <u>know</u> where I came from and where I am _____; but you do <u>not know</u> where I come from and where I am _____."

John 10:14b–15a — "I know My _____, and am <u>known</u> by My own. As the Father <u>knows</u> Me, even so I <u>know</u> the Father."

John 14:7 — "If you had <u>known</u> Me, you would have <u>known</u> My _____ also; and from now on you <u>know</u> Him and have seen Him."

Being "born of the Spirit" means that we have Christ's Spirit in us. I ask little children sometimes, "When you asked Jesus to come into your heart, you didn't open up your chest and put little, bitty Jesus inside you, did you?" They almost always smile and say "no", but one little kid said, "Yes, I did!" She, her parents, and I had a long talk before I baptized her!

Jesus defines eternal life as "knowing God intimately" in John 17:3, *"And this is eternal life, that they may <u>know</u> You, the only true God, and Jesus Christ whom You have sent."* Eternal life doesn't begin when we die. It begins with an intimate knowledge of Christ.

Pray this prayer to God: *"Our Father in heaven, as I am growing to know You, the only true God, and Jesus Christ, whom You sent, help me to live for You each day. Thank You that I have been born again into Your family. In Jesus's Name I pray. Amen."*

DAY 6: MORNING
New Belief: Believe In The Only Begotten
(Read John 3:13–21)

What does John 3:18 explain as the condemnation that will keep a person from eternal life with Christ? Is it that if a person is morally evil, he will be condemned? Or, is it that if a person does not *believe* in the name of the only begotten Son of God (Jesus), he will be condemned? Jesus told Nicodemus that we are already judged and condemned because we are sinners. Faith is the only way to avoid condemnation.

In whom do we believe? The only Begotten Son. The word literally means "only generated Son" and is different from believers who are children of God by faith. While you may become a child of God, Christ is the only One who actually *is* God in the flesh. We on the other hand are adopted into becoming children of God.

For you did not receive the spirit of bondage again to fear, but you received the <u>*Spirit of adoption*</u> *by whom we cry out, "Abba, Father."* (Romans 8:15)

But when the fullness of the time had come, God sent forth His Son, born of a woman, born under the law, to redeem those who were under the law, that we might receive <u>*the adoption*</u> *as sons. And because you are sons, God has sent forth the Spirit of His Son into your hearts, crying out, "Abba, Father!"* (Galatians 4:4–6)

His unchanging plan has always been to <u>*adopt us*</u> *into His own family by bringing us to Himself through Jesus Christ. And this gave Him great pleasure.* (Ephesians 1:5, NLT)

Read John 3:20. Have you considered sin (anger, lust, worry, envy, etc.) as hatred toward God, the Light? On the other hand, obeying God manifests your love for God. John 14:21 says if we truly love God, we will keep His commandments.

Various translations render John 3:36 differently. They either say anyone who *"does not obey"* (ESV, NASB) or anyone who *"does not believe"* (NKJV) will not see life. The Greek word is not the typical word for either "disbelief" or "disobedience" and could be translated as *"refuses to believe"* (HCSB). Whatever the reasons for the different translations, there is a connection between believing God and having life, and refusing to believe God and not having life.

You cannot love sin and love God at the same time. Are you persuaded by the only Begotten Son of God? If so, you will show your love through faith in your obedient actions.

Pray this prayer to God: *"Dear God, take away all judgment of my sins. Strengthen me to refuse to practice evil. Instead, help me to do what is true in response to Your love for me. Amen."*

DAY 6: EVENING
New Behavior: Christ Must Increase, We Must Decrease
(Read John 3:22–36)

You might think that John the Baptizer would be "tempted" to be jealous of Jesus. However, his entire life was preparing the people to hear from Jesus. Of all people, John the Baptist would have been the *last* person to be jealous of Jesus. When he baptized people, he immersed them in much water (verse 23), getting the people totally wet to signify their total repentance, or turning away from their sins. But he knew there was going to be a greater baptism.

He said "the Lamb of God" would baptize with the Holy Spirit (John 1:33) and with fire (Matthew 3:11; Luke 3:16). Fire purifies by burning off the bad and leaving the purity God wants for us.

> ### 2 Timothy 3:12
>
> Yes, and all who desire
> to live godly in
> Christ Jesus will
> suffer persecution.

Like a loyal best man in a wedding, John knew the Bridegroom had come for His bride. He was not jealous of Jesus, but some people were instruments of temptation. They came and said, "He who was with you is baptizing … and all are coming to Him." Even though we are "born again," we can still be tempted, and we can still sin.

"He must increase, and I must decrease."

John knew what Jesus was doing was right. The Baptizer eventually would be put in prison and be beheaded for his convictions (Luke 3:18–20). John willingly suffered for the sake of righteousness, and we also need to be prepared for temptation and suffering.

Have you suffered since you have come to Christ? Have you experienced doubt? Persecution? Temptation? Read Romans 8:18–39; 2 Timothy 3:12; and 2 Corinthians 12:7–10 to encourage you to "decrease" as you face adversities in your life as a Christian so that Christ can "increase."

Ask God to continue to create opportunities for you to spend time daily with Him in prayer and Bible reading. If you have not been baptized (that is, totally immersed in water) after you have received Christ, decrease your resistance to His will, increase your obedience, and follow the Lord's command (Matthew 28:19) and example (Matthew 3:15) in this area of your life.

Pray this prayer to God: *"Lord God Almighty, give me insight to see things from Your heavenly perspective. Grant me the ability to have the mind set on the things of God and not on the things of human beings. In the power of Jesus Christ, I pray for Your glory, not mine. Amen."*

—John Chapter 4—

MEMORY VERSE:
"Whoever drinks of the water that I shall give him will never thirst.
But the water that I shall give him will become in him
a fountain of water springing up into everlasting life."

(John 4:14)

In John 4:26, we see the first of seven "I AM" statements with no direct object (also called the "Stand Alone I AM Statements" or the "Intransitive I AM Statements") which could be considered bad grammar, but for Jesus it is great theology. To say "I am tired", "I am a teacher", or "I am going to tell Jesus He used bad grammar" makes sense. But when Jesus says "I AM," you need to know that "I am" in the Hebrew is the equivalent to the name *Yahweh* or Jehovah and in the Greek, it is *ego eime*. In each of these "I AM" statements, Jesus is telling us who He is.

εγο ειμε

He is Personal in our relations.
"I AM that speaks to you."

John 4:26

In the Old Testament, Jehovah God would reveal Himself and distinguish Himself from the other "so-called" gods who were made out of wood which did not speak or do anything (see Psalm 115, for instance). When Jesus came to the woman at the well, she was surprised that a Jewish man would speak to her, a woman with a questionable reputation. Today, many are surprised that the God of the universe would speak to them. As I write this, I am in awe that God forgave my sins and puts up with me. I love Him and He "walks with me and He talks with me and He tells me I am His own" (*In the Garden*, hymn published 1912). The idolatrous images made in the Biblical days did not have a personal relationship with those who worshipped them. We, on the other hand, have a God whose presence is with us always, who invites us to pray to Him, and responds when we do.

εγο ειμε

He is Perfect in love.
"I AM, do not fear"

John 6:20

Jesus next uses the "I AM" phrase (in Greek, *Ego eime*) in the context of fear. The disciples saw Jesus as he walked on the storm. His response to their fear was *"I AM, do not be afraid"* (*Hebrew Names Version*). From the beginning, our response to a holy God is fear. Adam in Genesis hid himself from God because he was naked and afraid. Jesus walks on the storms of life and provides deliverance. His perfect love drives out all fear (1 John 4:18).

εγο ειμε

He is Preeminent in judgment.
"If you do not believe that I AM."

John 8:24

Thirdly, John reveals the "I AM" in the context of a lack of faith or unbelief. The doubters were mocking Christ because they knew His mother became pregnant when she was not married. They did not know who His physical father was, not realizing that it was more important who His *Heavenly* Father was. The *lack* of faith that Jesus is the "I AM" is what causes God's judgment of unbelievers. By faith alone in Christ and His sacrifice, they could avoid the punishment. Jesus declares in their presence three times (8:24, 28, 58) in this one chapter that He is "I AM," that is, "Yahweh God." He declares that lack of faith will cause them to miss eternal life.

εγο ειμε

He is Provider of salvation.
"…you will know that I AM"

John 8:28

The fourth "I AM" statement is a reference to the cross. When Jesus is lifted up on the cross, He was fulfilling the true Passover, bearing the sins of the world. Jesus said that on that day that He is lifted up, they will know that He is who He said He was. Some may have come to salvation on that day, while others in full knowledge, rejected Him still. In this passage, Jesus was asked who He was, and as a result of this "I AM" statement, many placed their faith in Him (see John 8:30–31).

εγο ειμε

He is Perpetual in existence.
"Before Abraham was, I AM"

John 8:58

This was the clearest "I AM" statement, as Jesus boldly stated that He existed before Abraham. He proclaimed He was Yahweh, existing before and was greater than the Jewish spiritual father Abraham. As a result, the Jewish people picked up stones to hurl at this blasphemous "prophet" as they presumed Jesus to be. British Professor and Writer C.S. Lewis, author of the Chronicles of Narnia and numerous Christian classic books, put it perhaps the most succinctly: Jesus was either a liar, lunatic or the Lord He claimed to be.

εγο ειμε

He is Prophecy fulfilled.
"You may believe that I AM"

John 13:19

The context here is faith in times of doubt. The disciples were about to go through what would undoubtedly be the darkest time in their lives—those hours between the betrayal and the resurrection. When Judas revealed himself as the traitor he was, the disciples needed to know that this was a part of God's plan. It was not just Jesus who predicted this to come about. One thousand years earlier, in Psalm 41:9, God foreshadowed that a close friend who ate bread with the Messiah would lift up his heel against Him. When we have times that test our faith, God wants us to know He knows the future, He is in charge of the future, and He prepares us for it.

εγο ειμε

He is Power over all.
Jesus said to them, "I AM"

John 18:5

The final "I AM" declarative statement shows that Jesus is more powerful than man's armies or soldiers, more powerful than betrayal, and through it all, the great "I AM" can cast any opposition onto their backs. God is sovereign, and no one can oppose Him. He could have called more than twelve legions of angels (Matthew 26:53). At the mere utterance of His statement "I AM", the soldiers fell backwards. One day, just as Judas and the soldiers fell, every knee shall bow, and every tongue shall confess He is Lord.

DAY 7: MORNING
Questions: How To Dodge The Smoke Screens
(Read John 4:1–18)

In John 4, we see Jesus in active witnessing. The woman's thirst was more than merely physical. She came to draw water at mid-day, a time when most other women would not come due to the heat of the day.

When the discussion comes around about her life and need of a Savior, she quickly turns the conversation to a theological debate that was being argued at the time. This is called a "smoke screen" which people often bring up to hide the fact that they need to get right with God.

Here are a few "smoke screens" which are brought up today to turn conversations into theological debates:

"Why are there hypocrites in church?"
"What about the people who have never heard about Jesus?"
"Isn't the Bible filled with contradictions?"
"Where did Cain get his wife?"

All of these have satisfactory answers for sincere seekers, but none of those answers will meet the need of receiving God's forgiveness and direction in life. Ask yourself if you have heard a few other "smoke screen" questions that you may have encountered as you tell others about Christ.

Not all questions are smoke screens. You may have legitimate questions about Christianity…I know I do! May I offer you some encouragement: There is no question that you have that other thinking and wondering Christians have not already asked, and yet they still have faith in God. Even if you come up with a question no one has ever asked or one that no one has ever adequately answered, rest assured that God has an answer.

More importantly, our questions, answers and lack of answers do not dethrone God. The best answer perhaps to almost every question is simply this: Because there is a God!

Pray this prayer to God: *"Dear Lord God, give me the boldness to cross traditional, racial, economic, and denominational boundaries in my love and care for others. Give me wisdom on when and how to answer a skeptic's question. In the name of Jesus I pray. Amen."*

Day 7: Evening
Pride And Prejudice
(Read John 4:19–24)

Jesus frequently used the natural surroundings to turn the conversation into a spiritual parable. The "water" that Jesus offered the woman was free for the asking (4:10), completely satisfying (4:14a) both internally and eternally (4:14b).

When the disciples returned, they revealed some prejudices not seen in Jesus. Have prejudices ever stopped you from talking to someone of a different race? Would you be more likely to witness to someone of your same gender? Do you avoid talking to someone about God because they are too poor? Too rich? If you met someone and discovered they were in an immoral lifestyle, would you tell them about God?

It may have been difficult to honestly and personally answer some of the questions above. If so, ask God to rid any prejudice you may have. Make a commitment to seek out people who are different from you to share Christ with.

Some people use John 4:21–24 to justify not going to church. "You don't have to go to church to be a Christian," they often say. But that was not what Jesus was saying. More accurately, Jesus said God seeks a worshipful attitude in spirit and truth, wherever and whenever you may be worshipping, including in a public worship setting. In fact, being with others helps you avoid a selfish, solitary spirit. Worshipping with others also helps you stay in the truth. Being with other believers helps you avoid the error of possibly creating "God in your own imagination."

There is something good and holy about worshipping God *with* other people which takes away our pride. It is humbling to come before the awesome Creator of the universe, especially when you are surrounded by other fallible human beings. It is easy to be loving and kind when we are by ourselves, but God wants more than that!

Worshipping God in a local church is a vital part of your Christian growth. Notice that immediately after this conversation, the woman wanted to find the very people whom she previously had been trying to avoid. She wanted to seek them out and bring them to Jesus. Pride and prejudice make you run from people. Humility and love make you run to others with the good news, the gospel.

Pray this prayer to God: *"God, I repent of my sin of not worshipping You in spirit and in truth. Help me see that true spiritual worship is found privately and publicly with You and with others You love. In Your name, I will humbly submit myself to the loving care of others in the church. Amen."*

DAY 8: MORNING
Come and See: The Power of a Witness
(Read John 4:25–42)

After talking with Jesus, the woman's priority was no longer getting water…she left her water pot with Jesus. Jesus had quenched her spiritual thirst. Jesus also had His needs for food met. Read verses 31–34. What do you think Jesus meant?

Notice that the woman's message was similar to that of Philip when he found Nathanael in John 1:46. It was also the invitation Jesus gave to John and Andrew in John 1:39—they simply said, *"Come and see."*

Our job is to bear witness. God is responsible for the results. Some people may say, "Witnessing is not my gift." But based on 4:35–38, we cannot know what will happen when we simply go tell people about what we know of Jesus.

It is like planting seeds. A person who plants is no less important than the one who reaps or the person who tends to the crops. Look at verses 34–38 and take note of how important it is for us to plant, tend, and harvest the "crops" in God's harvest field. Look around you. Is the need for harvesting any different today than it was in the time of Jesus?

The woman could have used all types of excuses to not go and tell the people of the town about Christ. Now, the woman who came to draw water when no one else was around wants to share the Living Water with everyone.

How did God use the woman's witness in verse 29 to get people to come to Christ? Read verse 39. The woman's radical change was the very thing that God used to make the people interested! What does that say to you about how God could use *you* and your testimony to reach others with the good news?

"Many more believed because of His own word." If God blesses you with a harvest, remember it is Christ, not your testimony, which saves. Verse 42 seems hurtful. "We no longer believe just because of what you said." It is helpful to remember that if we tell others about Jesus, it is up to them and up to God on how they respond. Don't wait until you are all polished and perfect to share your story. They cannot respond unless we share the simple message of "Come and See."

Pray this prayer to God: *"Heavenly Father. Take away every excuse I have for not serving You and telling others about You. Give me power as I live my life so that others may come to Christ. I will give You all praise and glory and honor. In the name of Jesus I pray. Amen."*

DAY 8: EVENING
Faith: Seeing Is Not Always Believing
(Read John 4:43–54)

I once shared Jesus Christ with a teenage girl. She eagerly received the "good news" about salvation. She asked Jesus to come into her life, to forgive her sins, and to clean up her life. The tears she shed were genuine tears of joy because of her new life. She was so excited when she went home to tell her family. Despite her joy, their reaction was as cold as the Arctic Ocean. "Oh," her father said, "you'll grow out of that stage."

If you have received Jesus Christ as Lord (He is in charge) and Savior (He has delivered you from sin and death), do you feel like you are a new person?

If you have not received the support for your faith from home or friends, read verse 44. Jesus not only cares, He understands! He has been there. He knows what it is like to be misunderstood. Every believer will face doubts and opposition.

John recorded the second "sign" in his gospel and again it occurred in Cana. Jesus obviously did more miraculous signs than John records (verse 45). In reality, God could simply have shown so many supernatural signs of His power that everyone would be forced to "believe." God's desire is for us as Christians to grow in faith, despite opposition or obstacles, and sometimes, in absence of "signs."

Twice the nobleman insisted Jesus to "come down" and heal his son. Jesus put his faith to the test by telling him to *"Go your way, your son lives."* God wants you to grow strong in faith in the midst of opposition. *"Unless you see signs and wonders you will not believe."* Believe in Jesus even if it seems no one else will.

John records only a few miracles, and yet this one is not recorded in any of the other gospels. Why is it significant? It is important in that it comes right after a statement that a prophet is without honor in his own country (Nazareth).

Although it was a part of Galilee, Nazareth was skeptical of Jesus. People were skeptical of Jesus because He was from there. A king's official and the "wicked Samaritans" believed on Him, yet not his hometown, nor his home people. Jesus is the Savior of the world and not just the Jews. In fact no one can come to the Father except through Christ (see John 14:6). Read 1 Peter 4:12–13. Don't believe in God because of your surroundings. Believe in spite of your surroundings.

Pray this prayer to God: *"Oh, Lord My God. Give me faith to trust in You, whatever comes my way. I place my faith in You and You alone, not in my circumstances, not in what I can or cannot see, and certainly not in how many others around me believe. I put my trust in You. Amen."*

—John Chapter 5—

MEMORY VERSE:

*"Most assuredly, I say to you, he who hears My word
and believes in Him who sent Me has everlasting life,
and shall not come into judgment, but has passed from death into life."*

(John 5:24)

(NOTE: See Luke 1:5–25; 39–80; 3:1–22 for a background on John the Baptist)

"Yeah, we were related and everything, but it was not like we grew up together. My folks were old and lived in Jerusalem, and his folks were, well, they didn't have a whole lot of money for traveling, if you know what I mean. Joseph was a carpenter in Nazareth and my father was a priest. We just didn't run in the same circles.

"There was a time when I remember Jesus came to Jerusalem. I was about 13 and my father had already died but my mother Elizabeth was still being cared for by the other priests and their wives. It was probably the only time I ever saw Him as a kid.

"But even then, He wasn't a kid. I guess I was going through a rebellious time in my life and I really did not want to hang out at the Temple with all those 'old guys.' I thought, 'My cousin Jesus is coming to town? Finally, somebody my age.'

"So, when Joseph, Mary, and Jesus finally got here, what does He want to do?! He wants to hang out with all the old guys at the Temple. Not fun! I hate saying it, but I always thought, 'As soon as Mom dies, I'm getting as far away from Jerusalem as I can!' But Jesus … it was like He couldn't get enough about God. I didn't get it then, but now I do!

"My mom always told me about my 'miraculous birth' and His birth too, but when I was a kid, I just thought it was typical Mom stuff. You know, 'my son John is a special child. He was born after an angel appeared to my Zacharias in the Temple.'

"But when I met Jesus, it was like all that she and Abba had told me was true. He really was different. But as a kid, I thought He was different … but not in a good way.

"Long story short, our paths came back together when I was preaching down south on the Jordan River. I was telling people to repent and I was baptizing and preaching away.

"You heard me preach it, John: *'The Messiah is coming, and He will baptize people with the Holy Spirit and with fire.' 'He is the Lamb of God. He will take the sins of the world away.'* All this time, I was thinking *'This Messiah is going to be something else. I won't even be able to unstrap His sandals.'*

"And what do you know? Would you believe it? Guess who it is? My own cousin!

DAY 9: MORNING
Deliverance: Do You Want To Be Made Well?
(Read John 5:1–9)

John 5 begins with *"After this, there was a feast of the Jews..."* This was likely one of the feasts in which Jews were encouraged to go to Jerusalem. The first one after Passover was Pentecost which occurs <u>seven</u> weeks after Passover. That would make sense, as this miracle occurred on the Sabbath or the seventh day. Or it could have been the Feast of Trumpets or the Feast of Booths. Whichever feast it was, some time had passed since Jesus had left Jerusalem at Passover.

When Jesus encountered the lame man, He asked him a strange question: "Do you want to be made well?" He knew the answer, but Jesus asked questions like these to make the hearers (and us today) think. Of course the man wanted to be made well.

Like a "find and replace" function on a document, "find" the following elements and "replace" them with the spiritual truths below:

Find	Replace with
Great multitude	All of humanity
Sick people	Sinful humanity
Blind, lame, etc.	Sin
An angel stirring the water	False promises of salvation
The man with the infirmity	Those needing Christ
Efforts to reach the pool	Humanity's efforts to earn our salvation

The man was helpless to heal himself, putting his faith in his own efforts in a false belief. For thirty-eight years, this attempt failed again and again. Like the lame man, we are helpless to save ourselves. Putting faith in our efforts is just as useless as the man trying to get to the water.

After his healing, suppose the man had said, "Wow. I can wiggle my toes. I have feelings in my legs. I believe I can walk. But I am going to stay right here and keep trying to make it into the pool." His healing would be just as meaningless as us having our salvation and not walking in it.

The takeaway from today is "if you always do what you've always done, you'll only get what you've always gotten." Put your faith in Christ.

Pray this prayer to God: *"Lord, I do want to be healed. Help me to stand with You spiritually and for what You stand for, just in the same way the lame man was able to stand physically. In Jesus's name. Amen."*

DAY 9: EVENING
Grace: What Would the Father Do?
(Read John 5:9–24)

May I confess a sin to you? I know this is wrong, but it relates to today's story. When I drive to church and see people out running or doing the lawn, I sometimes judge them. I should pray for them that they would get into a Bible-believing church, but I often don't. I often do not even worry for their souls. I wrongfully judge them for not going to church.

Today's story is about religious leaders who saw a lame man walking and did not glorify God. Those leaders were spiritually paralyzed. They kept the Sabbath but got angry that Jesus violated the religious laws.

Obedience to God, like salvation, is by grace. Hebrews 10:19–35 speaks about the relationship between the *assurance* of our salvation, which is only by God's grace, and our *obedience* to God, and that too is also to be by His grace.

Bethesda, where the man was healed, means "House of Grace." God's grace not only saves us, it also helps us to walk in freedom from sin. Jesus told the man to "take up his bed and walk" and to walk in sin no more. If God has grace, we too should have grace on others when they have fallen. And we should walk our faith in grace.

John 5:21 is the first of seven comparisons of Jesus to God the Father. Jesus said "as the Father…so do I." They are:

1. *"As the Father raises the dead"* (John 5:21)
2. *"As the Father has life in Himself"* (John 5:26)
3. *"As the Father knows Me"* (John 10:15)
4. *"As the Father has told Me"* (John 12:50)
5. *"As the Father commanded Me"* (John 14:31)
6. *"As the Father loved Me"* (John 15:9)
7. *"As the Father sent Me"* (John 20:21)

I want people to go to church. But to be angry with people or to judge them who may not even be saved is wrong. Instead, I should tell them how to become a child of God. After all, isn't that what the Father would do?

Pray this prayer to God: *"I glorify You, Father, for liberating me from my sin by Your gracious gift. Help me to live for You and testify of You, no matter the cost. Like the lame man, help me to sin no more and then share Your grace with others. Amen."*

DAY 10: MORNING
Forgiveness: Past, Present, and Future
(Read John 5:24)

Read verse 24 out loud. *"Most assuredly, I say to you, he who hears My word and believes in Him who sent Me has everlasting life, and shall not come into judgment, but has passed from death into life."*

This verse shows me that Jesus has forgiven all the sins of my past, present, and future. Match the questions with the appropriate verb tenses.

___1. *"Has everlasting life"*		**A. Past**
___2. *"Shall not come into judgment"*		**B. Future**
___3. *"Has passed from death to life"*		**C. Present**

Using the New King James version, does this verse say a believer "will someday in the future pass from death into life" (future tense) or "has passed from death into life"?

Does this verse say a believer "will someday have everlasting life" (future tense) or "has everlasting life"?

Does this verse say a believer "shall not come into judgment" or does it say, "a believer probably won't come into judgment as long as he doesn't sin again"?

These past, present, and future tenses affirm to us the assurances of our salvation, our eternal life. When people are asked if they have eternal life, they may "think so," or "hope so," or think "maybe so." God wants us to "know so." Jesus said "most assuredly" (*"I'm telling you the truth"* –Good News Bible).

Another way to look at our salvation is "We were saved" (Justification); "We are being saved" (Sanctification); and "We shall be saved" (Glorification). Three theological words with deep meaning are explained below.

Justified. We have passed from death to life. Someone has said being justified is like being "just as if I'd never sinned." Even more than that, the word literally means God declares us and sees us as righteous (see Romans 3:22 and 2 Corinthians 5:21).

Sanctified. Day by day, the believer becomes more and more holy or "set apart" because he or she "has everlasting life."

Glorified. There will be a day in the future when we stand before God. On that day, we "shall not come into judgment." Instead, we will forever be separated from sin.

Pray this prayer to God: *"Jesus, Thank You for following the Father's example. Help me follow Yours. Remind me every day that there is nothing that can separate me from Your love and the love of the heavenly Father. Amen."*

DAY 10: EVENING
Listen To Jesus
(Read John 5:24–30)

Read again verse 24 from this morning's reading. You may ask yourself, "How can I already pass from death into life? I have never died." Did you know that before we became Christians, we were "spiritually dead?" Genesis 2:17 says that when Adam and Eve ate the fruit, they died spiritually. God is the source of all life (John 5:26) and our sins separate us from God. We are spiritually dead until we are brought to life through faith in Christ.

The phrase in verse 25 "the time is coming and has now come" means that from the time of Jesus through today, spiritually dead people, even though they are physically alive, will hear the voice of the Son of God and live.

The phrase in verse 28 "Do not marvel" can be loosely paraphrased as "and that ain't all." Not only does Jesus give life to the spiritually dead, He also states that ALL (from Mother Teresa to Adolf Hitler) in the graves will hear His voice.

If they have "done good" (that is, believe in Jesus, as explained in verse 24), they will be resurrected to everlasting life. See John 6:29 where Jesus even described believing as "a work of God. (Day 14: Evening).

To "have done evil" means if you have ever done anything that was bad. In other words you can be a mostly good person, but if you have done anything bad you will be condemned.

On the Day of Judgment, all will hear the voice of Christ. Every knee will bow and every tongue will confess He is Lord. But for those who are raised for the resurrection of condemnation, it will be too late.

The worst thing you can do is to reject God's gift of eternity. Revelation 20:12 speaks of two resurrections: If you are in the Book of Life, you are saved from condemnation. No wonder John wrote, *"Blessed and holy is he who has part in the first resurrection. The second death has no power over them"* (Revelation 20:6).

However, *"anyone not found written in the Book of Life"* are judged by their works and every one of those people will be *"cast into the lake of fire"* (Revelation 3:15).

Have you heard the voice of Jesus calling? Listen to Him. Later in John 10:27, Jesus will say *"My sheep hear My voice, and I know them, and they follow Me"* (see also 10:3, 8, and 16). Listen for Jesus today and follow Him.

Pray this prayer to God: *"Thank You, Heavenly Father, for giving me a firm assurance that Jesus is Who He said He is. Thank You for assuring me of my eternal life. Help me to listen to His voice every day. In Jesus's Name. Amen."*

Day 11: Morning
Testimonies Of Jesus!
(Read John 5:31–47)

In today's reading, Jesus gave five testimonies which gave witness that Christ was the Son of God (see 5:31–32, 33–35, 36, 37–38, and 39). On Day 2 (evening), we read how John wrote about two witnesses. Jesus, John the Baptist, the miracles, the Father, the Scriptures, the disciples (12:17; 15:27; 19:35; and 21:24), and the Holy Spirit (15:26) are all witnesses. There is room for one more witness: <u>YOU.</u>

Despite all of these witnesses, the real reason the religious leaders did not believe in Christ was because they didn't have the love of God in their hearts (5:42). Sometimes we think that if we say all the right words or have the best arguments that there will be some method and everyone would believe. However, salvation is not a matter of evidence or Scriptural arguments. It is not solely a matter of facts but simply a matter of faith.

Christianity requires faith but it is based on facts and not outrageous fables or outright fiction. There are things in the Bible that would be impossible if there was not a supernatural God.

People today and in the time of Jesus believe or "received" things which require faith but may or may not be true (see verses 43–44). In the margin, write down things which require faith, both things that are true and things that are ridiculous. As people of faith, Christians must trust in God, Jesus Christ, and the Bible, which is the only reliable testimony for us to know about God.

Some people say they believe in the God of the New Testament but not the God of the Old Testament. According to verse 47, if you do not believe in the writings of Moses, which includes the first five books of the Bible, can you say that you believe in the words of Jesus?

YES or NO

The Father and the Son are One (John 5:30). Both Testaments are reliable witnesses of Christ. St. Augustine said, "The New Testament is *veiled* in the Old and the Old Testament is *unveiled* in the New." Another has said "The Old Testament is the New Testament concealed, and the New Testament is the Old Testament *revealed*. Take God and His witnesses at their word.

Pray this prayer to God: *"Dear God, I stand and join in the testimonies that Jesus is the Son of God. I testify that I have Your love in my heart. I give a witness that I will believe You and what You have said in Your Word, the Bible, and in Your Word, the Lord Jesus Christ. In His Name I pray. Amen."*

DAY 11: EVENING
Jesus's "I AM" Statements, Signs, and Significances
(Read John 6:35,41,48,51)

John knew that others, such as Matthew, Mark, and Luke, had written gospels about Jesus. John reflected on Christ's life, recording the most significant events and teachings, including the seven "I AM" statements.

In Exodus chapter 3, Moses asked God, *"When they ask me 'What is the name of the God who sent you?' what shall I say?"* God told Moses to say, *"I AM WHO I AM. Thus you shall say to the children of Israel, 'I AM has sent me to you.'"* In the Greek version of the Old Testament, Exodus 3:14 was translated with the phrase *ego eimi* or I AM WHO I AM.

The connection between the seven I AM statements and the seven signs given in John are sometimes clearly linked and other times not so obviously connected. The link between "I AM the Bread of Life" and the sign of the feeding of the 5,000 is obvious. When Jesus said, "I AM the Light of the World" and the sign as He healed a blind man is also clearly linked. The connection between raising Lazarus and "I AM the Resurrection and the Life" is indisputable.

> **Exodus 3:13-14**
>
> In the Hebrew, the name of God, "Yahweh" or "Jehovah" and "I AM" are from the same root phrase, showing the eternal relevance of God to every generation.

The healing of the nobleman's son led his entire family to faith and is linked to "I AM the Way, the Truth, and the Life" (John 14:6) which is surrounded by encouragements to believe. The first miracle of turning the water into wine occurred at a wedding. It is linked to the final "I AM" statement: I AM the True Vine (John 15:1, 5) which calls us to bear fruit.

The paralyzed man was healed by the Sheep's Gate (John 5:2) and is connected to the statement of "I AM the door of the sheep." Jesus is God's door to the "house of grace," the translation of Bethesda. "I AM the Shepherd" is almost the exact phrase of Psalm 23, "The Lord (I AM) is my Shepherd." His protection is paralleled to His walking on the stormy sea, calming the waves, and dispelling the disciples's fears.

Jesus is the Great I AM in human form. His words need to be heard and heeded. His salvation must be believed and received.

Pray this prayer to God: *"Thank You, Father and Son, for being the Great I AM, the God who is Right Now. Thank You for being the God of the living and not of the dead. In the Name of the Great I AM I pray. Amen."*

—John Chapter 6—

MEMORY VERSE:
But He said to them, "It is I; do not be afraid."

(John 6:20)

I always feel a little sorry for Andrew and Philip. They should be a little more prominent, but they are not. James and John are the right and left hand-men of Jesus (at least that was what their mother wanted) and Peter is front and center. But Andrew, Simon Peter's brother, is of course going to fade behind his brother's persona.

And Philip? He seems to be a little off on the side. According to John's gospel, Philip is the third disciple called, after John and Andrew depart from being a part of John the Baptist's disciples. Philip and Andrew are really the first "go getters" literally. Andrew gets his brother Simon and Philip gets Nathanael. All are from the town of Bethsaida.

In Chapter 6, we can see a little of Philip's personality. The only miracle (other than the resurrection) found in every gospel is the feeding of the 5,000 with five loaves and two fish. It's likely that the miracle occurs in Philip's home town and so Jesus asks Philip a leading question as a test. *"Where can we go to buy bread so these can eat?"*

Jesus has no intention of buying bread, and to Philip's defense it was more of a "misleading" question. Yet Philip sees the physical not the spiritual. He sees what they <u>don't</u> have, not what they <u>do</u> have. We saw it earlier when Philip described Jesus to Nathanael. Whereas Andrew tells Peter, *"We found the Messiah,"* Philip describes Jesus as *"of Nazareth, son of Joseph."* Later, when the Greeks specifically seek out Philip to meet Jesus, he goes first to Andrew. Despite being with Jesus so long, Philip doesn't know Jesus very well, even on the final night before His crucifixion (see John 14:8–9).

In this longest chapter of the gospel, we will see that prayer was important to Christ and therefore it should also be to us. Through Christ we can conquer doubts and fears. We will see the significance of Jesus walking on water, and how to make our lives count for God.

By now in your walk with Christ, you have undoubtedly encountered some hard sayings that Jesus said. Despite His hard words, no matter our fears, our storms, and the "manna of this world" which leaves us hungering for more, this truth will always remain: Jesus has the "words of life."

Simon Peter got that truth. But Philip? It seems he is still a work in progress.

And aren't we all?

DAY 12: MORNING
Satisfied: Jesus Feeds 5,000
(Read John 6:1–14)

The feeding of the 5,000 is certainly remarkable. Every one of the four gospels, Matthew, Mark, Luke, and John records it. But it certainly was not the greatest miracle. All four gospels also report that twelve baskets of bread were left over. What do you think would be the greatest reason all four gospel writers chose to include this miracle?

1. It shows that Jesus can do really cool miracles.
2. It proves that the Bible can't be trusted because five loaves and two fish could never be enough to feed 5,000 people.
3. It teaches that Jesus doesn't want people to go hungry.
4. None of the above. Why do you think it was so important?

Many people remember that Jesus fed 5,000 with five loaves and two fish, but they have never stopped to think about why this story is so important. Read another reporting of the miracle in Matthew 6:5–12.

What would have happened if the young boy had not been willing to share his meal? Why was he the only one who shared? What can God do with what you have (physical abilities, singing, finances, friendships, experiences, learning, etc.) if you would give it to Him?

Read John 6:14 and compare it to Deuteronomy 18:15–18. The Jewish people knew Moses brought manna to the people. The gospel writers undoubtedly were making the connection between Jesus and Moses. Read 2 Kings 4:42–44. Jesus fed more people with less food than Elisha did. The writers were showing that Jesus was greater than the prophets. In Luke 11:31 and Matthew 12:42, the writers recorded Jesus as being even greater than King Solomon. Yet Jesus had a greater plan than becoming an earthly king.

Even deeper, Jesus later explained that He gives spiritual food that satisfies for eternity. While the people ate and were satisfied temporarily, the spiritual food Jesus offered satisfies forever.

Pray this prayer to God: *"Jesus, take what I have and use it for Your glory. Work a miracle through me. Let me be like Andrew and bring people to You. Let me be like the boy and share the little I have, so that You can make it much for Your Kingdom. Thank You for meeting and supplying all my needs. In the name of Jesus I pray. Amen."*

DAY 12: EVENING
Prayer Power Overcomes Peer Pressure
(Read John 6:15)

As you prepare for today's devotional on prayer, look up the following verses to go along with John 6:15. Matthew 14:23; 26:36–44; Mark 1:35; 6:46; 9:28–29; Luke 5:16; 6:12; 9:28. Jesus believed in prayer!

God created us to have fellowship with Him, so prayerlessness is certainly no small omission. Even if you do great works but do not cover them in prayer, that may reveal selfish motives or too much reliance on yourself. You may be seeking your own glory.

When the multitudes tried to "take (Jesus) by force," they were trying to make Him do something that was not in God's plan. His response? He left them all and went to pray.

Even though Jesus was and still is God, when He was here in the flesh, He needed to pray in all of His temptations, especially in response to what the crowd was wanting Him to do. Today, we call that temptation "peer pressure," and it does not only affect children and the youth.

Stop right now and pray. If you feel the pressure of the crowds to do something you know is against God's will, consider taking more time than usual in your prayer life. (These prayers given at the bottom of the pages are to get you going and are not meant to be the entirety of your prayers.)

If you don't know how to pray, you are not the only one—the disciples asked Jesus to teach them to pray. That was when He gave them the model prayer or sometimes called the "Lord's Prayer" (see Luke 11:1–4). Tell God you love Him. Confess any sins His Spirit may bring to mind. Ask for strength to do His will. Ask for your needs as well as your desires or requests. Thank Him for all that He is and all He has done.

And then pray for the strength to turn peer pressure into prayer power.

Pray this prayer to God: *"Dear God who hears my prayers, teach me to pray. Help me to seek Your face moment by moment. As I face trials today, give me the power and strength to fight my battles first in prayer. Thank You for answering each and every prayer. In the name of my Lord and Savior Christ Jesus I pray. Amen."*

DAY 13: MORNING
Step Out In Faith To Conquer Fear
(Read John 6:15–21)

How do you cope with fear? It is interesting that one of the most common greetings that angels and Jesus made was "Do not be afraid."

Today's passage (Jesus walking on the water) is the fifth of seven miraculous signs recorded by John. After reading John 6:15–21, read Matthew 14:24–33 for another perspective. Now that you have read it from two eyewitnesses, imagine yourself as being Simon Peter.

The fact that John did not record Peter walking on water is not surprising. John was selective in what he did and did not include in His gospel. His purpose was to draw attention to Christ, not anyone else.

> **1 John 4:18**
>
> *There is no fear in love; but perfect love casts out fear, because fear involves some form of punishment. But he who fears has not been made perfect in love.*

For the life of me, I can't imagine what prompted Peter to say he wanted to walk on those rocky waves in a pitch-black night during the middle of a storm. Maybe this was something the life-long fisherman had always wanted to do. This was certainly a first!

When I crossed Galilee the first time in 2004, the west side of the lake was so calm, it looked like a mirror. In the short amount of the time it took to get to the east side, the waves were coming across the bow. The storms of life can come just as quickly, but Jesus walks above them and beckons us to join Him by faith.

Jesus allayed their fears by saying "I am! Don't fear." This is the second time that John used this intransitive "I AM" statement. (See Chapter 4 Introduction)

The coupling of the feeding of the 5,000 with Jesus walking on the water should have proven to the people that Jesus was the Anointed One, the Messiah, also translated as the Christ. It proved to the disciples that He had power over all of creation. When the dark storms approach and overtake you, remember Jesus is "I am."

Pray this prayer to God: *"Thank You Father for being bigger than all my problems and stronger than all my fears. I praise You God that You don't give up on me, even when I sink. Help me to be willing to get out of the boat and take steps to conquer my fears through faith in You. In Jesus's Name I pray. Amen."*

DAY 13: EVENING
What Is To Be Learned Here?
(Read John 6:15–21 with Matthew 14:24–33)

When you were in school studying poetry, did you ever have to interpret what the poet was trying to say?

While the miracle of walking on water is great, let us not miss the message behind the miracle. In Mark 6:52, the writer says, *"They did not understand, because their hearts were hardened."* Don't have a hard heart.

When Christ comes into your life, He is strong enough to conquer any fear. Once the fear subsided, we see in Matthew that Peter became emboldened to walk toward Christ.

While we can criticize Peter because he began to sink (Matthew 14:30), remember eleven other disciples were too afraid to even get out of the boat. When Peter looked at Jesus, he walked on water. But when he looked away, he became afraid and started to sink.

If you are in a "storm" of your life, if the waves are crashing down on you, LOOK! Jesus is stronger than any storm. He is walking on top of the waves that would overwhelm any human. He is coming to help! If you have taken your eyes off Jesus, if you are looking at things that make you fear, cry out to Jesus, "LORD SAVE ME!" He will lift you up.

Jesus later said in John 14:27, *"Peace I leave with you, my peace I give unto you: not as the world gives do I give to you. Let not your heart be troubled, neither let it be afraid."*

Once Jesus got into the boat, the ship was immediately at the land. Without Christ, they rowed with great difficulty against the storms with great fear. With Christ, they went the distance by His power.

Pop Quiz: What is the writer trying to say? Be like the disciples and receive Christ (and his power) *"willingly"* (KJV), *"gladly"* (RSV), *"eagerly"* (NLT). Jesus, like a poet, used circumstances of life as symbolic teaching tools. See what the Master Poet is trying to tell you.

Pray this prayer to God: *"To the Christ who walks on the storms of life: Beckon me to walk with You, as I fix my gaze upon You and not on the waves, the wind and the worries of this world. In the name of Jesus I pray. Amen."*

DAY 14: MORNING
Make Your Life Count!
(Read John 6:22–27)

My mother died when she was 35, and my dad died a day before he turned 34. I was in college when I realized that if I only lived to be their age, two-thirds of my life was over. I decided then to make my life count.

Jesus sent His disciples across the sea without going on the boat with them. He went up to the mountain to pray, and then walked on the water to reach them in the middle of the night. No wonder the people were amazed!

Read verse 26 again. The people followed Jesus for selfish reasons and sometimes others (not us!) go to church for the wrong reasons. There is some "food that perishes" and some "food" that endures to eternal life.

A man asked a plumber, "What line of work are you in?" The plumber replied, "I serve Jesus Christ as my occupation. I just work as a plumber to pay my bills so I can continue my main job." Whether you are a writer, a custodian, a roofer, a pizza deliverer, an administrator, sales person, a fast food employee, a teacher or a minister (all of these are jobs I have held!), work for the "food," that will last for eternity.

Before you end today's devotional, pay attention to the last phrase in verse 27. Today, organizations set their seals on products to assure their quality to the consumers. Whether it is the USDA, Good Housekeeping, or the Better Business Bureau, people seek out those seals for product approval.

In the Bible days, bread bakers would set their "seal" of approval on their products. When Jesus performed the miraculous sign of the multiplied bread, the people saw this as God's "seal of approval" that He was a true prophet (John 6:14).

God wants your life to count for Him. Just like God put a seal on Jesus, He also puts a seal, the Holy Spirit, on you to make your life count. See 2 Corinthians 1:22; Ephesians 1:13; and Ephesians 4:30. Don't waste your life.

The death of my parents at a young age continually reminds me of the fragility and shortness of this earthly life. The reason for this book and your salvation is to remind you and others of the eternality of our spiritual lives.

Pray this prayer to God: *"Dear God, show me today what is important and what is not. Don't allow me to waste time on the temporary things. Show me what will last. Help me to seek You, not for what I can get, but for what I can give to You. Amen."*

Day 14: Evening
Work The Work Of Faith
(Read John 6:28–40)

What really pleases you? A sports team? Food? Your family? The Bible says that there is one thing that pleases God and in fact without this one thing, it is impossible to please God. (Hint: see Hebrews 11:6.)

What is this one thing? It is faith, also called belief or trust, in Him. The people asked how they also could do the works of God (6:28), wanting miraculous power. His response was not what they wanted to hear.

What "work" did you have to do in order to become a child of God? Did you have to give all your possessions to the poor or did you have to get baptized? Did you have to join a church or memorize a section of the Bible? Only one "work of God" is the greatest of all miracles: Believing in Jesus (verse 29). The greatest disobedience to God is the sin of unbelief (see Hebrews 3:17–18 and Hebrews 11:6).

Jesus said to work for the things that last eternally. Some followed Him, not because He had the words of life, not because He was the Son of God, and not even because of the miracles. They followed Him because He met their temporal needs. These immature followers would soon turn away.

If God never did anything miraculous in your life except give you salvation, would that be enough? Read John 6:35. Jesus performed two signs here (multiplying of the bread and walking on water), yet they did not believe in Him. Remember the woman at the well? He performed no sign with her, yet she believed.

God does not reject anyone who comes to Him in faith. The only people God will reject are those who refuse to believe that Jesus alone will save them. The work which saves is the "work of faith."

Ask yourself again, what pleases you? Hopefully, God pleases you and meets your desires, not for what He does for you, but simply because of your faith in Him. And that faith is exactly what also pleases God.

Pray this prayer to God: *"Dear Lord God, I come to You today in faith. Give me the confident assurance that You will live through me today. By faith in You alone, I will seek to do the work that will endure forever. Amen."*

DAY 15: MORNING
Who Can Hear These Words?
(Read John 6:41–58)

Strong words can be hard to listen to. They invariably only have two possible responses: strongly liked or strongly disliked.

This passage is difficult, so set aside some time to "digest" it well. Many took Jesus's words in this passage to be literal (verse 52), yet Jesus Himself says in verse 63 that the words are "spirit and they are life," meaning that they are to be interpreted as spiritual truths about eternal life.

The Jews were strong on religious rituals to gain God's favor. Yet here was Jesus, claiming anyone could have eternal life through faith. If you do not know for sure whether you have eternal life, it is either because you have not been taught adequately or because you are putting your faith in something other than or in addition to the work of Christ on the cross.

According to 6:47, if you believe in Christ, you have eternal life.

Jesus's first miraculous sign recorded in John's gospel was turning the water into wine and the fourth sign was the miracle of the bread being able to feed 5,000. Below are the elements of Communion (or "the Lord's Supper") and how they relate to elements in the Christian life. Draw a line from each element to its symbolic meaning:

1. The Cup	**a. Jesus's "Blood"**
2. The Bread	**b. Dying to Self**
3. Sacrifice	**c. Jesus's "Flesh"**
4. Service	**d. Living for God**

See answers below.

Today's passage does NOT teach that we receive eternal life through Communion. Instead it shows the spiritual *application* of what Christ did for us and how we can receive the benefits of His life and death through faith.

Pray this prayer to God: *"Heavenly Father. I have placed my trust in You, and I know that I have eternal life. Just as my body gains nourishment from eating physical food, I will nourish my spiritual life through You. Amen."*

1.a.; 2.c.; 3.b.; 4.d.

DAY 15: EVENING
You Have The Words Of Eternal Life
(Read John 6:59–71)

Do you have a spiritual journal, or a book to write down your thoughts about your spiritual life? Get it or a piece of paper for this devotional.

Are there things in the Word of God that are hard to hear or hard to understand? Are there things which even offend you? If so, write down some hard things that you don't understand or things which seem offensive.

Jesus asked those who were offended by His teaching what they will say on the day when He ascends back to heaven, which would prove that what He said was true. In other words, if anyone was offended that day by Jesus and then came and saw Him ascend to Heaven 40 days after His resurrection, imagine what they would say. Have you ever known Christians who were faithful to God at one time, but now no longer walk with Him, like those in verse 66? Write down some reasons why people stop living for God.

> **Eternal Life**
>
> The phrase "Eternal Life" or "Everlasting Life" is used interchangeably nearly 50 times in the New Testament and is explained in John 17:3.

When people stopped following Christ, He did not chase them down and apologize. He did not rephrase what He was teaching so that no one would be offended. And He did not get His feelings hurt. He asked the rest of the disciples who else was going to leave.

Verse 66 can be translated as *"Do you wish to leave also?"* The Lord was not asking out of depression or despair. He was saying that if anyone else wished to leave, they should go. A rough paraphrase of Peter's response is, "You're the boss, Lord. We're with you all the way to eternity."

No matter what the cost, don't let anything turn you away from Jesus. He alone has the words of eternal life (verse 68). Make a fresh commitment to God to continue to study His words, no matter the cost. Commit yourself to hear the words of life from Jesus as recorded in the gospel of John.

Pray this prayer to God: *"Dear Lord, I commit myself to stay with You, even when the going gets tough. I pray that my faith in You will never fail. Thank you that even if and when I am faithless and falter, You remain faithful to pick me up again. Thank You for not giving up on me. Amen."*

—John Chapter 7—

MEMORY VERSE:
*"He who believes in Me, as the Scripture has said,
out of his heart will flow rivers of living water."*

(John 7:38)

One of the hardest things to do is to listen and obey the Lord, when it seems He is whispering to us (if that!) rather than listening and obeying the world, when it seems it is shouting to us. Jesus had the same struggle and often withdrew to pray. Chapter seven brings us to the final year of our Lord's life, and Jesus faces some serious challenges. There are lessons to be learned for new and old believers, including how to know God's Word (doctrine), God's Will (discernment), and God's Ways (discipleship).

If you watch the movie *The Gospel of John* you will see Jesus speaking boldly. Perhaps this chapter will give you courage to speak boldly, despite opposition. In the previous chapter, we saw about God's spiritual food, and in this chapter, we see about the living water, quenching our spiritual thirst, and also reviving those whom we influence through Christ. This theme of living water is not a new theme, but a fulfillment of a very old theme, reaching as far back as Moses in the Old Testament.

You are a third of the way through this study. Keep going and learn more about your faith.

DAY 16: MORNING
Don't Listen To The World
(Read John 7:1–13)

There are plenty of distractions in the world: social media, ear buds, satellite radio. From sun up to sun down, constant sounds from the world can distract us from hearing from God. Though different, distractions existed in Jesus's day, tempting even Christ from His mission.

John 7 is in the fall of the year, the time of the Feast of Tabernacles. Jesus had withdrawn to Galilee because the Jews sought to kill Him in Jerusalem. Christians must have wisdom in knowing God's will and timing.

Does it surprise you that the Lord's brothers did not believe in Him (7:5)? Unbelievers, like Jesus's brothers, try to put Christians in a mold that doesn't fit. There are no cookie-cutter Christians. That is why our faith is a personal relationship with Christ. Don't be surprised if unbelievers try to tell you what a Christian is or isn't. Instead, listen to God!

Other things will also distract us. Frequently John wrote about Jesus's time (verses 6, 8) or His hour (2:4; 7:30; 8:20; 12:23; 13:1; and 16:21), usually in regard to His death. It is possible to do the right thing at the wrong time and only discernment and the prompting of the Holy Spirit will help in waiting on God's timing. See Isaiah 40:31; Psalm 25:3; 40:1.

In verse 8, most readings include the word "I am not going to the festival *yet.*" Jesus intended to go to the Feast, but just not *yet*. His brothers were pressuring Him to do something He was not ready to do.

The world today tries to squeeze us into its mold by getting something that is not in God's timing "yet." There are get rich quick schemes (lotteries), instant success books, credit cards, prayerlessness, sex before marriage, and countless other pressures to distract from God's will.

I listen to audio books. I love playing D.J., picking out music for the day. And everyone knows I am a news junkie. But there are times I have to be still before God and tune out the world and listen to God.

Pray this prayer to God: *"Heavenly Father, help me to wait for You. No matter what the world says, help me to always call on You first before making any decision. Help me also to listen for Your answers, especially when Your answers are different from the world's desires or even and especially my own desires. Amen."*

DAY 16: EVENING
Do Listen To God
(Read John 7:11–24)

People have never had a "middle-of-the-road" opinion about Jesus. In the 1970s, there was a song called *Jesus is Just Alright With Me*. Despite its popularity, the song is not very accurate. Jesus stands as a mountain peak. You can be on one side and agree with Him, or on the other side and disagree. Or ignore Him completely. But He can never be just alright.

Verse 16 uses a word, "doctrine" which we don't use often. It means teaching, usually according to a system of beliefs. In Christianity, we are to follow the doctrine of Christ. But how can we know true teaching?

To know truth, first notice Jesus's standard. He said that His doctrine was not His own, but from God (verse 16).

Unless you are perfect (and none are), true doctrine does not begin and end with you. In humility, you must admit that you are not the standard of truth, only God is. He reveals His perfect will in His Word, the Bible.

Jiminy Cricket's advice was "Let your conscience be your guide." But John 7:17, tells us our guide should be truly seeking God's will. That is how we can tell what true doctrine is. What are some pitfalls in allowing an imperfect conscience or public opinion to guide you in right and wrong?

If you want to find true teaching, you must not only seek God, but also have the right motivation. It is possible for you to read God's Word and distort it to fit your own purposes. That is the making of a cult.

The religious leaders selectively misapplied God's Word to Jesus. When you make a judgment on whether a teaching is true or false, it must line up with the doctrine as taught by the entire Word of God. 2 Timothy 3:16 says, *"All Scripture... is profitable for doctrine, for reproof, for correction, for instruction in righteousness."*

The three-prong test for true and correct teaching is: "Does this teaching lead me to do God's will?" "Does this teaching motivate me to glorify God?" and "Does this teaching line up with the entire Word of God."

Pray this prayer to God: *"Heavenly Father, guide me as I seek the truth. You alone are my standard. Help me to do Your will for Your glory as I read Your word and apply it to my life. In Jesus's Name. Amen."*

DAY 17: MORNING
Speak Boldly Despite Opposition
(Read John 7:25–36)

When I was an editor of a south Texas newspaper, I had a coworker who knew I was a Christian, but she was not. When the subject of Christianity arose, she told me, "Oh, I know Jesus." One time I told her, "You know *about* Jesus, but you don't *know* Him personally."

People were divided on whether Jesus was good or a deceiver. In verses 25–27, the people were not seriously asking whether the rulers were believers in Christ but rather they were taunting the inability of the rulers to respond to Jesus.

The religious leaders knew of Jesus's earthly background, but they were ignorant of the spiritual power behind Him (see John 9:29). They also were ignorant of where Jesus was going (verses 33–36). They knew Jesus was of Nazareth, a place from where no prophet arose. They also knew that he was from humble means, that He had never formally studied (verse 15). Since Jesus was not born with an earthly father (Luke 1:35), some implied Jesus was born of fornication (John 8:41) and called Him a Samaritan (a slang for a mixed-race person) in John 8:48. Despite His background, Jesus spoke boldly to the powerfully respected and esteemed rulers.

We too know where we are from and where we are going and that should give us the boldness to testify. Opposition to the truth and lack of true knowledge should lead us to be bold in our proclamation, because others truly need someone to stand up for what is true.

The guards were asked "have you ever known of ... one Pharisee to believe in Him?" Nicodemus and Joseph of Arimathea were there (John 7:50–52, John 19:38–39) but were afraid to speak boldly. **Imagine what would have happened if two Pharisees had been bold!**

Acts 4:13–31 shows the source of the disciples's boldness. *"Now when they saw the boldness of Peter and John...they realized that they had been with Jesus."* We should not look to ourselves for the boldness to witness for God, but rather we should spend time with Christ in order to give us God's power and boldness.

Pray this prayer to God: *"My Father in Heaven, as I spend time with You, give me boldness to speak strongly about You, not just around my Christian friends or at church, but to go out to where there is opposition and unbelief. In Jesus's Name I pray. Amen."*

DAY 17: EVENING
Faith In Jesus Will Quench Your Thirst
(Read John 7:37–53)

The **"Great Feast"** likely was the Feast of the Tabernacles. The feast reminded the Israelites of when they had lived in tents or "tabernacles," wandering in the desert before entering the Promised Land. This feast reminds Christians that we are living in earthly tabernacles, inhabited by the Spirit of God (1 Corinthians 3:16; 6:19).

The Jews had an elaborate water ceremony on the final day of the Feast, remembering that their forefathers thirsted in the desert and also that water flowed from a rock. Jesus used this time to proclaim He was the fulfillment of that ceremony.

Read 1 Corinthians 10:4: *"all drank the same spiritual drink. For they drank of that spiritual Rock that followed them, and that Rock was Christ."*

John 7 parallels Exodus 17:1–7. The people were thirsty in a dry place and asked Moses for water. They argued with him, asking *"Is the Lord among us or not?"* and were almost at the point of killing him. In Jesus's day, the Jews argued whether Jesus was the Messiah or not (verses 40–44), and like with Moses, some even sought to kill Him (verse 25).

Moses struck a rock with his rod and water flowed from it. Isaiah 53:4 says that Jesus was *"stricken, smitten by God, and afflicted."* The living water that flows out of Christ is the Holy Spirit (John 7:39), which God pours out on His people who trust in Christ.

The Old Testament speaks of living waters (Jeremiah 2:13; Psalm 36:8–9; Psalm 42). Isaiah 44:3 says *"For I will pour water on the thirsty land, and streams on the dry ground; I will pour out My Spirit on your descendants and My blessing on your offspring."*

The people were more concerned about where Jesus was from than who He was and what He had to say. God's concern with you is not where you have been, but where you are. He looks at what is within you, not what is behind you. From your "inner being" He will flow rivers of living waters.

Pray this prayer to God: *"Our Father in Heaven. Give me spiritual drink today. Allow me to be a source of life for others as I drink from You. No matter what others say, I will put my faith in You. In Your Holy Name I pray. Amen."*

—John Chapter 8—

MEMORY VERSE:
*"Therefore if the Son makes you free,
you shall be free indeed."*

(John 8:36)

We ended chapter 7, looking back at Moses when he struck the rock and water flowed. That living water was a symbol of the Holy Spirit. But later, in Numbers 20, we see a second time when the people needed water. This time, God told Moses to speak to the rock. Instead of speaking to the rock as God commanded, he struck it twice. As a result, Moses could not enter the Promised Land because he did not trust God and did not show God as holy to the people.

The lesson from that is that Jesus was struck once for our salvation. He finished the work on the cross and was raised from the dead. He is now seated at God's right hand. We never need to strike the Rock again, but we only need to speak in prayer to Him and He will pour out refreshing Spiritual water.

It is with that freedom we enter into chapter 8. New believers understand that Christ forgives them, but sometimes they find it hard to forgive themselves. Other times they find it hard to forgive others, despite Christ's forgiveness. The freedom to forgive and be forgiven is seen in the account of the woman caught in adultery, the freedom from the lies of Satan and the world, and the liberty not only from sin's punishment but also from sin's power.

We will see the recurring theme of light in this chapter and again in the next. We will learn about judging others as well as ourselves and what true judgment looks like. Sometimes we think judging people or their actions is wrong, but in Chapter 8, we will see that judging in comparison to ourselves is indeed wrong, but judging only against the God's standard of truth is right.

At the end of the chapter, we will make note of one of the strongest, boldest claims Jesus makes when he declares His deity and oneness with God in His "I AM" statement. We will also see how it gets the religious crowd riled!

DAY 18: MORNING
Don't Cast Stones
(Read John 8:1–12)

A church in California is very successful in reaching lost people for Christ by its contemporary style. Few come to church dressed with coats and ties and some unbelievers come hardly dressed at all. One of the surprising difficulties is that once the unbelievers come to Christ, they are quickly critical of how newcomers dress and act, even though they dressed and acted much in the same way before they became believers.

The accusers caught a woman in the very act of a sexual misconduct (we are not given the details of how they did this and or why they did not bring the guilty man before Jesus). They saw an opportunity to trap and embarrass Jesus with a very difficult situation.

> **1 John 1:9**
>
> "My sin" may be different than your sin but it is no bigger nor smaller than yours. We as Christians need to be ashamed of "my sin" regardless of whether it is socially acceptable.

Many wonder what Jesus wrote on the ground but since the Bible does not tell us, there is no way to know for sure. More importantly, notice why Jesus wrote on the ground: to make it seem "as though He did not hear them." They kept pushing Him for an answer, and so He straightened up, answered them, and then stooped back down and again played in the sand! Jesus sure knew how to get people to pay attention.

From a human perspective, some sins are definitely worse than others (I certainly would rather someone get angry with me, even without a cause, than to murder me). But from God's perspective, all sins are grievous sins. Can you imagine? These hypocritical religious leaders were trying to put the sinless Son of God to the test!

Jesus didn't condemn the woman, but He did command her "Go and sin no more." Only God can truly separate the sin from the sinner, but that doesn't mean we should not try separate those two as well. If I ever get to a point where "their" sins are bigger than "my" sins, I can rest assured that God will "doodle in the sand" until I am more grieved with my own sins than the sins of others.

Pray this prayer to God: *"Heavenly Father. I confess that the smallest of all my many sins is more important in my relationship with You than the biggest sins of my neighbor. Help me to look to You and never 'cast stones' at others. Help me instead to be an instrument used by You to tell others of Your love and forgiveness. Amen."*

DAY 18: EVENING
See The Light!
(Read John 8:12–30)

In this second Transitive "I AM" Statement, Jesus said "I AM the Light of the World." (To review, see Day 11: Evening.)

The most obvious benefit of light is that it allows us to see. It reveals objects that are there but are unseen or obscured. Darkness flees from the presence of the light. Have you ever entered into a house in the day when all of the lights were unnecessarily on? It usually means that someone left when it was dark and did not turn off the lights (or you live with teenagers!).

Lights are needed when there is darkness, and the greater the darkness, the greater the need for light. Those seeking to kill Jesus were only showing their spiritual darkness. Jesus confronted the darkness by boldly proclaiming the truth and brightly showing the light.

Had Jesus not been who He said He was, the following statements would have been on the verge of lunacy or profound egotism: *"He who follows Me shall not walk in darkness, but have the light of life." "You are from beneath; I am from above. You are of this world; I am not of this world." "If anyone keeps My word, he shall never see death." "Most assuredly, I say to you, before Abraham was, I AM."* (John 8:12, 23, 51, 58)

Jesus said He was the Light of the world and not just for Israel. A prophecy of the Messiah would be that He would be a Light to the Gentiles (see Luke 2:32). For more verses about the light, see John 1:4–9; 3:19–21; 9:5; 11:10; 12:35–36, 46; and 1 John 1:5–7.

Twenty-one times in this chapter alone, the word "father" is used. Jesus is the source of life (John 1:4; 8:12), and He is the only way to become a child of God. Only those who know Jesus (8:19), love Jesus (8:42), as well as believe in Jesus, and receive Jesus (John 1:12) are truly God's children.

Does that sound judgmental? The religious leaders thought so too. Jesus said His judgment and the Father's judgment was true (John 8:16). For more on truth, continue in tomorrow's devotionals.

Pray this prayer to God: *"Dear Lord Jesus, shine your spiritual light to me that I may see. As a moth is drawn to the light, draw me closer to You. In Jesus's name. Amen."*

DAY 19: MORNING
"The Truth Will Set You Free!"
(Read John 8:31–36)

Truth is a spiritual parallel to light. It exposes errors and lies. When Jesus said that He was the light of the world, the Pharisees denied the truth of this statement. Like a person awakened by a bright light, they "covered their eyes" and called Jesus a liar. Yet Jesus was the truth.

We often hear the phrase "the truth will set you free." This is not about academic knowledge, but faith shown by obedience in action to Jesus's words. The Apostle Paul speaks a great deal in Romans 6 about slavery to sin and freedom in Christ:

6knowing this, that our old man was crucified with Him, that the body of sin might be done away with, that we should no longer be slaves of sin. 7For he who has died has been freed from sin… 12Therefore, do not let sin reign in your mortal body, that you should obey it in its lusts…

16Do you not know that to whom you present yourselves slaves to obey, you are that one's slaves whom you obey, whether of sin leading to death, or of obedience leading to righteousness? 17But God be thanked that though you were slaves of sin, yet you obeyed from the heart that form of doctrine to which you were delivered. 18And having been set free from sin, you became slaves of righteousness.

> Read Romans 5:15

"Cheap grace is the preaching of forgiveness without requiring repentance, baptism without church discipline, communion without confession, grace without discipleship, grace without the cross, grace without Jesus Christ."
Dietrich Bonhoeffer

20For when you were slaves of sin, you were free in regard to righteousness… 22But now having been set free from sin, and having become slaves of God, you have your fruit to holiness, and the end, everlasting life.

Along with the forgiveness of sin, we are also given great freedom. Earlier in this chapter, Jesus set free the woman who was caught in adultery. She was freed not only from the judgment of her sin by the law, but also free to "go and sin no more."

Freedom is never free, but always worth fighting for. Believers are free from the penalty of sin, but not yet free from its presence. Until we are perfected in eternity, we must wrestle against the power of sin.

Pray this prayer to God: *"Dear God, help me to walk in freedom from sin. As Jesus taught us to pray, do not allow us to be led into temptation, but deliver us from evil. In His name we pray. Amen."*

DAY 19: EVENING
"I Am Telling You The Truth!"
(Read John 8:36–58)

Do you ever say the word, "AMEN"? In the Greek and Hebrew both, the word Amen means, "Truth".

In the Good News Translation (which is used in the film *The Gospel of John*), Jesus repeatedly says *"I am telling you the truth."* Other versions say, *"verily, verily"* or *"most assuredly."* In the Greek, it is "Amen."

The Pharisees were firmly deceived by a lie from the father of lies. Therefore, Jesus had to come out strongly and boldly. They thought that Jesus was not telling the truth (verse 13); they did not know what He meant in His teachings (John 7:36 and John 8:21–22); they did not know the Father or Jesus (verse 19); they did not see that were lost in their sins (verse 21); they did not know that their father was the devil (verse 44); and they did not know they were not from God (verse 47).

Notice verses 31–32. There are some conditions necessary in order to know the truth. Verse 31 says you must abide in His word and be His disciple. In other words, you must be doing what He has commanded, and you need to be following His example.

Have you ever come across someone who did not want to obey God's Word, but had a strong opinion about who God is? Many people who are living ungodly lifestyles are often the harshest critics of the church and Christians and are also the first to say they themselves are not so bad. They judge by "the flesh" (verse 15) or by human standards. God's standard, His truth, is the Word of God (John 17:17), and the contents and commands of God's Word.

The Apostle John tells us repeatedly that we are children of God and have certain privileges (see John 1:12; 1 John 3:1). One privilege is that we are able to stay in His house forever, just as the Son of God is able to stay in His Father's house forever.

The Pharisees were still so trapped in their own self-righteousness that they could not see their own need for forgiveness. Therefore, they were still in bondage to sin.

The truth of God's Word can free us from the bondage of sin.

Amen? Amen!

Pray this prayer to God: *"My Father in Heaven, show me the truth of Your Word today and help me to keep it in my life. Wherever there is falsehood in my heart or deeds, reveal to me how Your truth will free me. Amen."*

—John Chapter 9—

MEMORY VERSE:
*He answered and said, "Whether He is a sinner or not
I do not know. One thing I know: that though
I was blind, now I see."*

(John 9:25)

The last chapter spoke about light, this one speaks about sight. John Newton, a slave trader turned preacher and hymn writer, penned the words of *"Amazing Grace."* His songs were written out of a life of despicable sin, yet it was the very sins in which he was once mired that made his advocacy against slavery so very powerful. His words of "I once was blind but now I see," were not about him physically but each one of us can relate to the spiritual blindness we once had and now how we can see the truths of God.

In our study of Chapter 9, we will be confronted with perhaps Christianity's greatest and oldest question, "Why evil?"

We will also see our relationship with Christ and how He relates uniquely and differently with each of us. We'll see that there should be a change in us, a conversion, which makes us see things differently, but others will also see us differently. And we'll see ourselves differently, in a humbling way before an Almighty God.

In fact, we'll see, it is all a matter of, well, perspective.

DAY 20: MORNING
Why Is There Evil In The World?
(Read John 9:1–12)

Imagine or recall the joy of your first child. You now have a new life in the world, perhaps to make it a better place. It is a chance for a clean slate, a fresh start with a child untainted by the worries and problems we ourselves have experienced.

Perhaps you have personally experienced the shattering of those dreams as did the parents of the man who was born blind. As modern science has shown, the "sins of the parents" are sometimes passed down to the children. For example, an expecting mother who drinks alcohol can damage the child growing within her.

While deformities sometimes occur as a result of the misdeeds of parents or a genetic code, in this case Jesus said that the blindness was not a result of sin. Rather, the tragedy of the man's blindness was allowed so that the works of God could be revealed in him.

Read Romans 8:28

Only God can take the evils of this world, mold them into His own holy plan and produce good as a result.

God uses evil to show His goodness by contrast. Jesus's light is shown to expose how dark and sinful the world is. Our sins, our rejection of God, the effects of an imperfect world and Satan himself are all the sources of evil. But God uses all of these things to work together for good for those who love God and are called according to His purpose (Romans 8:28).

Without her blindness and deafness, do you think we would have ever known about Helen Keller? What lessons can you learn from her?

Fannie Crosby wrote 9,000 hymns and songs of praise to God yet was blinded by improper medical treatment. God didn't cause that evil, but He used it.

Only God could turn the worst tragedy in all of human history -- the death of Jesus Christ -- into the greatest triumph in human history. What can God do with the evil you have experienced?

Pray this prayer to God: *"Dear Heavenly Father, there are many things in this world that I do not understand. I know You are grieved far more than I could ever be with the evil that exists in this world. When evil falls my way, help me to trust You to make it through. Help me to see ways in which You will reveal 'the work of God' through it all. Thank You for being Lord in the good times and also Lord in the times of evil. Amen."*

DAY 20: EVENING
The Difference Between "Religion" And "Relationship"
(Read John 9:13–25)

The difference in religion and Christianity is that religion is humanity reaching to God. Christianity, on the other hand, is God reaching to humanity. Many have said "Christianity is not a religion, it is a relationship."

There is a viral video by Jefferson Bethke, who, while in his early 20s, used a spoken word poem to explain that thought. He later wrote a book entitled *Jesus > Religion: Why He Is So Much Better Than Trying Harder, Doing More, and Being Good Enough.*

Jesus doctored this man's eyes with saliva, dirt, and water. However, in other times, He only spat on the eyes (Mark 8:23), simply touched them (Matthew 9:29), or even just spoke a word (Luke 18:42) and healing occurred.

God ministers to us in different, personal, and unique ways. God is personal in His relationship to us. His complex nature is distinct to each individual. Yet He is still the same God. Don't fall into the trap of trying to make everyone understand God just like you do.

Compare the man's statement with the attitude of the Pharisees. *"One thing I know: that though I was blind, now I see."* Instead of giving glory to God that a man who was born blind was now seeing, the Pharisees were upset with Jesus for healing on the Sabbath day.

Many people get upset with fellow Christians because they don't "give glory to God" in the same way that they do. Even though God blesses both sides with followers, salvations, and growth, churches can split, and deep feelings can be hurt for years simply because Christians try to limit God's revelation of Himself.

We should guard against heretical doctrines which contradict the Word of God. Cults and false teachings have been around since the dawn of Christianity (Matthew 7:15), and every Christian must carefully study the Bible. But today's study reminds us to give room for God to be God. He is too infinite to be limited to our "box" we wish to put Him in.

Pray this prayer to God: *"Lord God, reveal to me today how infinite You are. Show me Your great expanse. Give me vision to see how beyond my limited sight and demonstrate to me how You reveal Yourself personally and uniquely to each of Your children. Guard my heart from falsehood and lead me in Your Truth. In Jesus's Name I pray. Amen."*

DAY 21: MORNING
A Changed Life
(Read John 9:26–34)

You cannot help but see the humor, irony, and even sarcasm in this story. Here, a man is healed from blindness since birth, and the enemies of Christ want to turn it around as a cause for accusation against Christ.

Consider your own conversion. Were there people who have been less than supportive to you as your life has changed?

"Why do you want to hear it again? Do you want to become His disciples too?" Imagine never having been able to see anything but darkness and suddenly having sight given to you. In modern times, several people have been cured of blindness, and it is always an overwhelmingly emotional event. And yet, here is this man and his family put immediately on trial.

While you may not have been delivered from physical blindness, in a very spiritual sense, all lost people are blind and when we come to salvation, it is like a light given to us that those who are spiritually blinded cannot see.

"Now this is remarkable…" (9:30, NIV). Could there be anything *more* remarkable than a blind man suddenly receiving his sight? The healed man appears to be saying that the refusal by the Pharisees to acknowledge both the miracle and the anointing of God on Jesus was even more remarkable than his healing.

To be cast out, as seen in verse 22 and 34–35, means to be "excommunicated" from the Jewish faith, to no longer be allowed to worship in the synagogue.

Since you became a Christian, have you experienced any shunning or being "cast out" from your family, your friends, your co-workers, even your church?

I can only imagine that when the Pharisees "cast him out" of the faith, the blind man literally looked around and kept on smiling as he left.

When we see how spiritually blind those around us are, we need to look at the eternity God has in store for us and then joyfully glorify God for His miracle in us. When we look at what the world has to offer us and compare that to His Spirit living within us, we just need to let His loving Light shine out.

Pray this prayer to God: *"Dear God. I pray for those who do not know You as Savior and Lord. I ask You to let my light shine before them that they may see my changed life so that they too may know You as I do. Even if they do not understand me, thank You for giving me sight to my spiritual blindness. In Jesus's Name. Amen."*

DAY 21: EVENING
To See, You Must First Admit Your Blindness
(Read John 9:34–41)

These verses reveal that Jesus healed the blind man not just to deliver him from darkness, but to show how dark sin truly is and how spiritually blind some people, even religious people, can be.

First of all, notice how the Pharisees continued to harass the man whom Jesus had healed. The Pharisees had become so blinded and so opposed to Christ that they did not know how ridiculous they sounded, even to the healed man (see his joking in verses 27 and 30).

Jesus cared for the man who was "cast out" and came personally to Him to comfort him. If you have been cast out because of your faith, know that Jesus has and will continually seek you out and encourage you.

Do you believe that the Pharisees "saw" themselves as sinners? (See verses 24 and 34). If true vision means being able to "see" yourself as a sinner in need of forgiveness, and if spiritual blindness means "seeing" yourself as being able to work for your own righteousness before God, then paraphrase verse 41 in terms of how unbelievers "see" and how they are "blind."

As you grow as a Christian, you will find that your spiritual insight is growing. You will not suddenly have all knowledge and all answers. In fact, learning more about Christ is part of the joy of being a Christian. I have seen new believers so hungry for God, it is as though they cannot ask the questions fast enough or read the Bible long enough to satisfy their spiritual hunger.

There is a verse in Proverbs that relates to the growth of a believer. *"The path of the righteous is like the first gleam of dawn, shining ever brighter until the full light of day."* (Proverbs 4:18, NIV). Don't lose your enthusiasm for growing. Keep reading this devotional book but more importantly, keep reading the Word of God.

Pray this prayer to God: *"Dear Jesus. Thank You for the forgiveness of my sins. I am absolutely helpless and blind without You. Keep my heart from pride and arrogance when I look at the sins of others. I believe in You and worship You as the Savior of my soul and the giver of sight to my true spiritual condition. Amen."*

—John Chapter 10—

Memory Verse:

"And I give them eternal life, and they shall never perish; neither shall anyone snatch them out of My hand.

(John 10:28)

The 23rd Psalm is and always has been a beloved passage of Scripture. Jesus knew that and used the illustration of Him being a shepherd and of us being the sheep. In Chapter 10, the mid-point of the gospel, we will glean from this study the ability to know when God is speaking to us. We will see our blessed assurance that God who saved us will keep us saved.

Our Lord once again declared His unity with the Father and once again the religious rulers sought His life. The main difference we can see between all of the various religions and Christianity is, "What do they believe and teach about Christ?" Only one religion teaches that Jesus Christ is uniquely the Son of God. Jesus never backed down from His statements to be God in the flesh. And yet, not only was Christ the Son of God, able to save, He was the Son of Man, able to relate with us.

It is marvelous that a shepherd would lead his sheep, but even more that a Shepherd would, in a sense, become a sheep so that the enemy would attack Him, rather than the rest of the flock.

DAY 22: MORNING
The Shepherd, The Sheep, And The Stealer
(Read John 10:1–21)

If you have ever stayed through the closing credits of a movie, it was likely to see one more video clip at the very end. In movies or on playbills for theatric performances, there are always listings of the cast of characters and the cast members. In today's reading, see if you can identify who the "cast of characters" are: the door (10:1, 7–9); the thief/robber (10:1, 10); the shepherd (10:2–4, 11, 14–16); the sheep (10:3, 11); strangers (10:5); the hireling (10:12–14); and the other sheep (10:16).

We start with the Door, the third "I AM" transitive statement. Sheepfolds only had one entrance, and sometimes without a gate, so the shepherd would actually sleep at the entrance and block any coming in or out.

The robbers are those who steal the sheep, by force or deceit. Jesus accused the religious leaders of being false teachings. Others want to kill the sheep or destroy the entire sheepfold.

Jesus plays a dual role in this cast: I AM the Door and I AM the good Shepherd. By His life, He is our Shepherd. By His death, He is our Door. Christians intimately know Jesus, follow Him, and know the Father through Him. A hireling is not a shepherd. When danger comes, hirelings will flee, but a good shepherd protects and gives his life for the sheep.

Strangers will lead sheep away if the sheep consistently listen to those other than the shepherd. This aspect of the parable stresses the importance of personal and corporate time of listening to Christ. It also reminds us not to go to the world for moral or spiritual teachings.

The sheep trust Christ as Savior. There is no other way to heaven except through Jesus (John 14:6). If anyone seeks to enter the sheepfold by any other door than Jesus, they are not sheep (Matthew 7:15). At this time, Jesus had only come to the Jews.

The other sheep are the Gentiles who would come to Christ later. All are Christians, since they only have "one shepherd". We all come to God the same way that Jesus had called His own people--by faith (Romans 1:16).

Pray this prayer to God: *"Savior, like a shepherd, lead me. You gave me abundant life by dying for me. I am Yours. Help me listen for Your voice alone in personal study and through teachers true to Your Word. Amen."*

DAY 22: EVENING
You Will Never Be Snatched Out Of The Father's Hand
(Read John 10:22–30)

The Feast of the Dedication, or Hanukkah, was in December, a few months after the previous section, but Jesus continues the analogy of the sheep and the shepherd. The analogy of the sheep and the shepherd reminded the people of God's faithfulness to keep His flock in the fold. If a shepherd would risk his life to save a sheep from a ravenous wolf, what would he do if a sheep wanders away? See Matthew 18:12–14 in another parable about a shepherd with 99 faithful sheep and one straying sheep.

Those who asked Jesus to plainly tell them if He were the Christ had no intention of believing in Him. What was the reason they did not believe in Jesus?

a) Jesus had not shown enough signs to convince them
b) He didn't make enough convincing arguments
c) They were not His sheep and would not follow Him, no matter what

Sometimes we think if only God will do something miraculous for people then they will become Christians. Christ has done all that needs to be done for them to believe, but the evidence is not so overwhelming that people do not have a choice. Still, we are commanded to witness (to tell others about Christ) and give "reason for the hope that is within you" (1 Peter 3:15), but their salvation is solely between them and God.

What's more, Jesus and the Father are one. Both the Father and the Son are agreed on the issue of your salvation. Don't miss this point (like the people did who picked up stones to stone Jesus). The point Jesus was making in saying no one will snatch you out is that if you are one of His sheep, you will follow Him, and you will never lose your relationship with God.

If Jesus went to the cross for you, faced down death and experienced the resurrection, He will not give up His fight for you, even if you fall back into your sins. The Bible says He is now at the right hand of God interceding for you (Heb. 7:25). To be snatched out of the Father's hand, the snatcher must be greater than both Father and Son. Neither you, your sins nor the devil is greater than the Father and the Son!

Pray this prayer to God: *"Lord, I commit my life to follow Your light. As long as You shine Your will clearly in my life, I will do my best to walk in Your time and in Your truth. Thank You for the precious promise that no one, not even me, can snatch me out of Your hand. Amen."*

DAY 23: MORNING
Is Jesus God?
(Read John 10:15–33)

Did Jesus ever proclaim Himself to be God? Today's passage is a clear proclamation from Jesus and those who heard Him. They were going to stone Him for His "blasphemy." But then Jesus quotes Psalm 82:6–7.

Imagine this: Jesus has always been God. He says He was the Son of God. The Jewish leaders then wanted to stone Jesus because He claimed to be God's Son, even though there are many Old Testament verses which say God is our Father (see Deuteronomy 32:6; 2 Samuel 7:14; 1 Chronicles 17:13; 22:10; 28:6; Psalm 68:5; 89:26; Isaiah 63:16; 64:8; Jeremiah 3:4; 3:19; 31:9; Malachi 1:6; and 2:10). Other times it is strongly implied: (see Exodus 4:22–23; Deuteronomy 1:31; 8:5; 14:1; Psalm 103:13; Jeremiah 3:22; 31:20; Hosea 11:1–4; and Malachi 3:17).

Whew! Did you look all those verses up? Didn't think so. That's okay, but if you ever want proof, there you have it! So, what does Jesus do? He exposes their ignorance even further by referring to a Scripture where God calls unrighteous humans "gods." We will discuss this more this evening.

Jesus also said the "Scripture cannot be broken." The Word of God is sure, and Jesus gave numerous statements which proclaimed that we could trust God's Word.

Just as an author can interject himself into his novel by having one of his characters say what he wants to say, so God came down to humanity by casting Himself as the part of Jesus Christ! John's gospel has numerous references confirming Jesus is God, but here are just a few of Bible verses outside of this gospel.

Matthew 1:23—*they shall call His name Immanuel…"God with us."*

Colossians 1:19; 2:9--*For it pleased the Father that in Him all the fullness should dwell. … For in Him dwells all the fullness of the Godhead bodily;*

1 Timothy 3:16--*And without controversy great is the mystery of godliness: God was manifested in the flesh, justified in the Spirit, seen by angels, preached among the Gentiles, believed on in the world, received up in glory.*

Hebrews 1:8 *But to the Son He says: "Your throne, O God, is forever and ever…"*

Pray this prayer to God: *"Heavenly Father, I confess that Jesus Christ is the true Son of God. Only by receiving Him could I be adopted into Your family. Help me to live out Your unbreakable Word of Scripture in my life. In Jesus's Name. Amen."*

Are We Gods?
(Read John 10:34–42)

Read Psalm 82, especially verses 6 and 7. There is only one God, the Creator of the universe. However, the Bible acknowledges there are false gods (little "g"), as explained by Paul in 1 Corinthians 8:4–6. Humans have responsibilities similar to what God has. The judges were sinful and did not exact true justice. God told these mortal humans "to whom the word of God came" that they were responsible for representing God to the world.

God asked, "How long will you judge unjustly and show partiality to the wicked?" He then commands the judges to *"defend the poor … do justice to the afflicted and needy …You are gods (elohim), and all of you are children of the Most High. But you shall die like men, and fall like one of the princes."*

There was no delusion that these were even godly judges, let alone "gods." But as God's representatives, they should have known better than to mistreat the poor, afflicted, and needy.

There is a phrase "You may be the only Bible some will ever read." Another is "You may be the only Jesus some will ever see." Those phrases don't mean you are a literal book or Jesus Christ. That was what the psalmist meant about humans being "gods." Sinful human beings have responsibilities akin to God, and yet they were going to stone Jesus for claiming to be the Son of God.

Unlike the judges in Psalm 82, Jesus was the *"visible image of the invisible God"* (Colossians 1:15), He was the manifestation of God in the flesh (John 1:14). He had the right to be called the Son of God. Jesus was not "proof-texting" the Bible to get out of a tough spot. He was saying (my paraphrase), "My Father, in His holy and unbreakable Word, said that sinful judges were to act like God. And you think it is blasphemy because I claim to be the Son of God?"

(I would even add in my paraphrase, "GIVE ME A BREAK!")

His answer did not and was not meant to calm them down, as evidenced in verse 39. It was a bold, declarative statement that He was the only begotten Son of God, equal with His Father in Heaven.

Pray this prayer to God: *"Dear Lord, I ask you to live in me today, so that I could be a good representation of You. Thank You for giving me Jesus Christ as an example for me to follow. In Jesus's Name. Amen."*

—John Chapter 11—

MEMORY VERSE:

Jesus said to her, "I am the resurrection and the life.
He who believes in Me, though he may die, he shall live.

(John 11:25)

At the core of Christianity is the resurrection. Paul said if there is no resurrection, there is no Christianity (1 Corinthians 15:16–19). In the next four sessions, we are going to learn about patiently waiting on God's timing, about five essential lessons on death and grief, and what to do when you come to the end of your faith.

The fifth "I AM" claim that Jesus made is the clearest in the connection between the miracle (the raising of Lazarus) and the message (that Jesus is the source of eternal life). It is noteworthy that three of the seven I AM statements speak of life: I AM the Bread of Life, I AM the Resurrection and the Life and I AM the Way, the Truth and the Life. Surely Jesus wanted to convey that He is Life Itself.

Mary and Martha knew Jesus could have done something to prevent the death of their brother, but He didn't. You too will experience that God is sometimes not what you think He should be and He acts in ways that you do not think He should act.

This chapter marks our half-way point in our seven-week journey. Keep going, knowing more and growing more in the Lord.

Day 24: Morning
When Following Turns To Fainting: An On-Time God
(Read John 11:1–6)

When Jesus left Jerusalem, the leaders sought to kill Him, *"but He escaped out of their hand."* Jesus had previously said He was not going to Jerusalem and for good reason. After the Feast of the Dedication of the Temple (Hanukkah), Christ went east, to the other side of the Jordan River, where John the Baptizer had earlier worked.

Even though John did not perform miracles, many believed his prediction that a greater One was coming after him. His witness of Jesus was shown true by Christ's *words* and miraculous *works*. John 10:42 says that many believed on Jesus there.

In Jerusalem, they wanted Jesus dead, yet just a few miles away, many were coming to salvation. Jesus knew His time on earth was short, and many were trusting in Him and responding positively there because of seeds sown by the Baptizer. No wonder Jesus did not go immediately to heal Lazarus!

Read 2 Peter 3:8-9

God always has his eye on the clock and his hand on the temperature control. His kiln will produce His desired outcome and in His perfect time.

Mary, Martha and Lazarus were still in the home of their father, Simon. They were perhaps not much more than teenagers. Jesus had a fondness in His heart for them, yet He prioritized His ministry. Sometimes your affections will tempt you to leave where you fully see God working in your ministry. As a result of Jesus staying, God received even greater glory than if Jesus had dropped everything and left.

When Jesus made the decision to go back to Jerusalem (Bethany is just east of the city), the disciples tried to talk Him out of it. Jesus responded in verse 9, *"Are there not twelve hours in the day? If anyone walks in the day, he does not stumble, because he sees the light of this world."*

The disciples knew the danger Jesus would be in by returning to Jerusalem (verse 16). But Jesus trusted God's perfect timing (that was likely what Jesus meant in not stumbling). When we pray for *God* to act or when He calls *us* to act, we need to look for His leadership. There's a phrase that says, "God may not always be on time, but He is never late." Trust God to answer your prayers in His time. Respond to God when He tells you to.

Pray this prayer to God: *"Lord, I commit my life to follow Your light. As long as You shine Your will clearly in my life, I will do my best to walk in Your time and in Your truth. Amen."*

When Friends Fall: Lessons From Death
(Read John 11:1–27)

When sickness or death comes, John 11 is a good passage to read. Readers will often rush to read about the resurrection of Lazarus, but there are several lessons that we can learn from death, sickness, and grief before we get to the chapter's climax.

Lesson 1 (verse 3): Death and affliction can be interceded for. We can pray for the sick and the dying. Sickness is not a result of bad karma. Sickness is not a state of mind from a lack of faith. James 5 says leaders should pray for the sick, and expect healing to occur (Mark 16:18).

Lesson 2 (verse 4): Death and sicknesses are instrumental for God's glory. If we do not see instantaneous healings, it may not because of a lack of faith, but because God seeks to glorify Himself through it all. The Bible says those who wait on the Lord shall renew their strength (Isaiah 40:31).

Lesson 3: (verses 6–10): Death is intentional. Jesus waited for Lazarus to die. God has a purpose in death, primarily to save us from this sinful world. Read Genesis 3:22–24--God purposely disallows us from living forever in this fallen state of sin. But if we walk with Jesus, His light will guide us, regardless of the circumstances around us (John 11:10–11). A frequent statement made by missionaries serving God is "The best place to be is in the center of God's will." Notice that the center of God's will is not always the safest place and being in God's will is not a guarantee that you won't encounter death. Being in God's will assure us of this: God will be glorified.

Lesson 4 (verses 11–15): Death is inevitable. Hebrews 9:27 says everyone will die. For a Christian, this earthly life is a small segment of eternal life and *"We are confident, yes, well pleased rather to be absent from the body and to be present with the Lord."* (2 Corinthians 5:8). Notice in John 11:15 that the death of Lazarus caused grief to Mary and Martha, but it caused Jesus to be "glad" because their struggle actually helped them to believe. Through adversity we grow stronger in our faith. Psalm 116:15 calls the death of His saints "precious" in God's eyes.

Lesson 5 (verses 16–27): Death is NOT invincible. Since death is guaranteed, we have cause to rejoice that Jesus has overcome and defeated it, and instead offers eternal life to us. The only way to beat death is to have a belief in Jesus Christ. Belief to the Christian is not just agreement, but it is an assurance, it is putting faith in the only One who can deliver us from death by beating death Himself.

Pray this prayer to God: *"Lord Jesus, help me to see Your working in all things, even adversity, sickness, and death. In Your name I pray. Amen."*

Day 25: Morning
When Faith Fails: At The Feet Of Jesus
(Read John 11:28–40)

Mary is frequently pictured at the feet of Jesus, while Martha is shown as busily working. John identified Mary as the one who would wash the Master's feet. There was another time when Mary was at the feet of Jesus. Read Luke 10:38–42. Which does Jesus say is more important, hearing from Him or doing for Him?

While serving God and listening to God are both important, we often want to work for God rather than listen to Him.

In John 11:21 and 32, the two sisters said the same thing so they likely had been complaining to each other about His delay. Martha "the doer" went to talk to Jesus, but "Mary stayed seated in the house." What emotions must Mary have felt?

Mary did not immediately go out to meet Jesus and her complaint indicates that she may have come to the end of her faith. While Martha professed her faith in verse 22, Mary's grief led Jesus to groan, weep and be troubled.

If Jesus wept, surely God understands that we too will mourn when we lose a loved one in death, even if we know they are in heaven. Jesus is the Resurrection and the Life and faith in Him is all we need to have life after death. Even still, grief at death is normal and was an emotion that even Jesus expressed.

Read 1 John 5:13. "*These things I have written to you who believe in the name of the Son of God, that you may know that you have eternal life, and that you may continue to believe in the name of the Son of God.*" What gives the Christian the confidence that he or she is going to heaven?

God's Word and our faith give us confidence in eternal life. If you have come to the end of your faith, there is only one place to go. Fall at the feet of Jesus. At His feet (that is, submit to God) we learn of faith. At His feet we declare our love. And it is at His feet we fall when we have nowhere else to turn.

It is one thing to profess your faith in Christ. But as Martha found, it is another thing when Jesus tells us to move the stone. Has God ever asked you to put your faith in action and actually do something for Him that might raise a stink?

If you want to see the glory of God, move that stone!

Pray this prayer to God: *"Jesus, I say with Martha, 'I believe that You are the Christ, the Son of God.' Give me faith when I face adversity, sickness and even death. Help me understand that Your delays are not denials, but preparations for greater deliverances. In Your name, I pray. Amen."*

When Funerals Are Not Final: Resurrection's Power
(Read John 11:41–57)

When Lazarus was raised from the dead, it was a symbol of Jesus's power of resurrection and the power of new life. One day, all believers will be raised up from the dead. It will not matter whether our bodies decayed, were cremated or were totally eliminated. The resurrection will be God's work and God's glory (verses 4 and 40). The hope of the resurrection should strengthen our faith every time we go to the grave or funeral of a believer (verses 15, 42).

Read 2 Corinthians 5:1–9. To be absent from the body (or in other words if we die), we are, according to verse 8, present with the Lord.

But before our physical death, Jesus also gives us life here on earth. When people come to faith, it is as though they have died to their old way of life and are raised to walk again in a new life (read Romans 6:4; 2 Corinthians 5:17; Galatians 2:20). We are to consider ourselves to be dead to sin, but alive to God. When Lazarus was raised, he was still bound hand and foot with grave clothes and his face wrapped with a cloth.

In a spiritual way, we who have been spiritually raised from our sins, should also shed our sinful "grave clothes." Just as Jesus said to loosen Lazarus from his clothes, we too should shed our clothes of death and sin.

> **Read Acts 2:22-23**
>
> *Jesus was delivered up by God's foreknowledge and determined purpose BUT by lawless hands for a wrongful death so that He could be raised again for our new life in His name.*
>
> **Regardless of circumstances, God always has the final word.**

Caiaphas, the High Priest, made a prophetic utterance that revealed the real reason why the Jews were so determined to suppress Christ. They were afraid of Rome and what it would do if someone like Christ would see to set up a different kingdom.

But in fact, one man did die so that the whole world would not perish. It was not the Jewish leaders who put Christ on the cross. It was all the sins of the world and according to the *"determined purpose of God."* (Acts 2:23)

Pray this prayer to God: *"Our Father in Heaven. Give me faith to believe that You have raised me from spiritual death and that when I face physical death, You will still be with me. Loosen me from my sinful nature and help me to walk in the liberty You have given me to live for You. Amen."*

—John Chapter 12—

MEMORY VERSE:
*"And I, if I am lifted up from the earth,
will draw all peoples to Myself."*

(John 12:32)

Of all of the chapters, I fear I have not written enough on the passages found in chapter 12. Prepare to spend a little more time and do not hurry through these rich and deep 50 verses.

Imagine if you will your beloved brother being raised from the dead by Jesus Christ. Martha, ever the serving follower, prepares the food, while Mary, ever the submissive follower, comes again to Jesus's feet. This time, she is not weeping with grief, but perhaps weeping with joy.

In these passages, look at the contrast between Judas and Mary; see the spectacle of Lazarus and the jealousy his being brought back from the dead raised within the chief priests; notice how Jesus receives the praise of children and how the people bore witness of Christ; pay attention to God's pleasure in the Greeks coming to Christ and who it was that brought them to the Lord; take note of the contrast of those who seek to save their lives and those who lose their lives; and don't miss the little verse that describes the rulers who believed but were afraid to confess their faith.

Jesus is about to be lifted up before the world, and in so doing, He will draw people to Himself.

DAY 26: MORNING
Give To God Your Very Best
(Read John 12:1–8)

A parallel reading of this account in Mark 14:3–9 and Matthew 26:6–13 says the anointing of Jesus's feet by Mary took place in the home of Simon the Leper. Knowing Jesus's healing power, perhaps it should read as "Simon the former leper." The anointing of the feet was a common practice and one with which Jesus was familiar (see Luke 7:36–50 for a separate event).

Mary is again at the feet of Jesus (see Luke 10:39; John 11:32), and Martha is serving. Mary anointed Jesus's feet with very expensive and fragrant oil. Other readings said she also poured it lavishly on the head of Jesus. Such an anointing was more than just simply cleaning the feet of an itinerant preacher. It was an extravagant ceremony and one that put Jesus in an extreme place of honor.

Have there been times when you were extravagant and lavish in your giving or ministering to God? Undoubtedly, Mary did such an act due to her appreciation of His raising her brother from the dead. But Jesus said that Mary had kept the oil for the day of His burial.

She probably understood what the disciples did not. Even if she didn't know Jesus was going to die soon, God called her, and He also calls us at times to do something extreme without fully knowing the reason why. And as in Mary's case, such giving can come with criticism.

Doing the right thing, like Mary did, can bring criticism, even from Christians. Remember the story of the widow who gave all that she had to God (Luke 21:1–4). Jesus did not rebuke her for giving, and He did not say, "No, you need that money more than God does." Jesus *praised* the widow for giving out of her poverty. Judas's criticism of Mary was shrouded with a ministerial covering; he appeared to be godly by saying he cared for the poor. Jesus's response did not mean that giving to the poor was unimportant, but rather we can give to the poor at any time (see Mark 14:7).

Like the widow and like Mary, God wants us to give Him the very best we have. Why? Because God wants us to be like Him. He too will give us His very best.

In fact, He already has! He gave us Jesus.

Pray this prayer to God: *"Dear Jesus, like Mary, I fall at Your feet today and seek to do Your will. Be glorified in my life today. Help me trust when I have little faith and help me in my unbelief. Amen."*

DAY 26: EVENING
The Whole World Has Gone After Jesus
(Read John 12:9–27)

This passage is often called the "Triumphal Entry." The other gospels record this event, but only John gives the reason for the celebration: the raising of Lazarus from the dead. The tremendous miracle of raising Lazarus from death and the response of the people is strikingly omitted from the other three gospels.

Assuming Mary, Martha and Lazarus were about the same age or even younger than Jesus, it is quite likely that they would have still been living when Matthew, Mark, and Luke were written (anywhere from 40 through 60 AD). Since the Jewish leaders in nearby Jerusalem wanted Lazarus dead, the other gospels likely did not mention this amazing event in part for Lazarus's safety.

The cries of the people that Jesus came "in the name of the Lord" fulfilled the prophecy from Psalm 118:25–26; His riding on a colt was prophesied in Zechariah 9:9. Imagine the confusion of the disciples of their Master, who formerly had refused anyone to tell others about His miracles, now was openly accepting praise and adoration!

It wasn't just Israel who came to Jesus. In 12:20–22, Philip and Andrew again brought people to Jesus. Recall that it was Philip who brought Nathanael to Jesus and Andrew who brought Simon (John 1:40–46). Andrew brought the boy with the five loaves and two fish (John 6:8). How about you? Have you, like Phillip and Andrew, brought someone to Jesus recently?

Three things happened that signified to Jesus that "His hour had come": (1) Gentiles began seeking Jesus (2) His triumphal entry to Jerusalem, and (3) Continued rejection from the religious leaders.

Previously, Jesus said His "hour" or His time to die had not yet come (John 7:6; 7:30; and 8:20). The hour for Jesus was when He was lifted up from the earth toward heaven on the cross. As a result, He would draw all nationalities, Jews and Gentiles (non-Jewish people), to Himself.

Do you seek to bring others to Jesus? Are you willing to lose your life, not by dying physically, but dying to your wants, desires and fears? Jesus said, *"Where I am, there My servant will be also"* (John 12:26).

Pray this prayer to God: *"Lord Jesus, like the multitude in Jerusalem, I have gone after You. Like the Greeks, 'I wish to see Jesus.' Give me vision to see beyond my limited sight. Show me how You reveal Yourself personally and uniquely to each of Your children. Amen."*

DAY 27: MORNING
Glorify Jesus!
(Read John 12:28–34)

The raising of Lazarus, the turning of the water into wine, healing the blind man, all glorified God, but nothing like the death and resurrection of Jesus from the grave. God's witness from heaven occurred at Jesus's baptism and at the transfiguration. Some heard God's voice, others heard an angel, and others only heard thunder.

"Glory" implies splendor and brightness and is linked with spiritual sight and light. In John's gospel, there are several ways God is glorified:

Faith or belief during adversity glorifies God. *Jesus said to her, "Did I not say to you that if you would believe you would see the glory of God?"* John 11:40

Answers to prayer glorify God. *And whatever you ask in My name, that I will do, that the Father may be glorified in the Son.* John 14:13

Bearing much fruit glorifies God. *By this My Father is glorified, that you bear much fruit….* John 15:8

Spirit-led proclaiming of truth glorifies God. *The Spirit of truth…will glorify Me, for He will take of what is Mine and declare it to you. All things that the Father has are Mine. Therefore I said that He will take of Mine and declare it to you.* John 16:13–15

To receive and believe His words glorifies God. *For I have given to them the words which You have given Me; and they have received them… And all Mine are Yours, and Yours are Mine, and I am glorified in them.* John 17:8, 10

Spiritual unity glorifies God. *And the glory which You gave Me I have given them, that they may be one just as We are one: I in them, and You in Me; that they may be made perfect in one…* John 17:22–23

Following Christ in death glorifies God. *This He spoke, signifying by what death he would glorify God.* John 21:19

In His sacrifice, rather than seeking God to deliver Him (John 12:27), Jesus asked God to glorify Himself. Sometimes we don't pray for God to glorify Himself, but instead we pray for God to "save me from this hour."

There is more to giving than just materially or financially. In 1 Corinthians 6:18–20, Paul says everything we have was bought by Jesus and we owe all to Him. What do you have to offer to Jesus that would ultimately glorify God?

Pray this prayer to God: *"Lord God, I give myself to You. I want all of my life to be a lavish gift to You. Help me to seek first the kingdom of God and Your righteousness. Everything else, I humbly receive as a gift from You. Amen."*

Day 27: Evening
Have You Seen The Light? Then Walk In It!
(Read John 12:34–50)

Do you wish that Jesus was still walking on earth today? The people who knew the Old Testament could not understand why Jesus was saying the Son of Man must "be lifted up," or in other words, die. But even while the light was with them, many did not believe (verse 37).

God does not want us to walk by sight, but rather by faith. God could live with us every day and demonstrate His power and His glory like He did in the Bible. But if He did, where would faith be? He could "force" us to worship Him by leaving us no choice. With that in mind, read verses 38 through 40 and see that God leaves us a choice to walk in the light.

In history, there were times when the "church" (not truly Christians) would threaten people to either profess faith in Christ or die. Such "faith" is not genuine.

In the same way, God could appear in the sky above and boom down from heaven, **"Believe in ME!"** but that would not give humanity much of a choice. In verse 37 John seems shocked that even though Jesus did so much and performed so many miracles, people still refused to believe.

What about you? In your walk with Christ, have you "seen the light"? Has God revealed Himself to you, and perhaps told you to "walk in the light"? Perhaps not audibly, but He will show you spiritual light in His Word.

Compare 12:35–36, 46 to John 3:19–21 and John 1:5–9. What are some similar characteristics of physical light and Jesus, the "light of the world"?

John writes elsewhere about what is one of the clearest evidences that you are walking in the light of Christ: Read 1 John 1:6–7 and 1 John 2:9–11, then write down what that evidence is.

When people don't want the light, they pull down the shades. If the sun comes from behind a cloud, a person preferring darkness may resort to getting even more shade. The same is true in the spiritual light. God wants to shine in the lives of people, but many would rather stay in the dark. The very presence of the spiritual light causes them to seek darkness all the more.

Pray this prayer to God: *"Father of Lights, shine down on me. I sometimes don't want to see the sin in my life and seek to keep it hidden. Help me to walk in the light and adjust my vision, so that I can see more clearly, the way You see all things. Help me to love others in Your light. In Jesus's Name. Amen."*

—John Chapter 13—

MEMORY VERSE:
*"By this all will know that you are My disciples,
if you have love for one another."*

(John 13:35)

The Bible says that Jesus held His "Last Supper" in a large upper room, perhaps the same upper room spoken of in Acts 1:13 where the power of the Holy Spirit came down. In this chapter, we see our Lord washing the feet of the 12 disciples, including the feet of Judas Iscariot.

Whether the washing of the feet was during or after the Supper, we are not sure (the Greek texts have variant readings). While we may not be sure on the time, we are crystal clear on its meaning: We are to serve one another. Jesus washing the feet also symbolizes the forgiveness He gave and how we are to forgive one another.

Chapter 13 begins a section on love that runs through chapter 15. Of the 39 times the word love is used in John, 27 times it is used in these three chapters. These are some of the most tender and intimate sections of all of Scriptures.

We see how we are to react when others, including those closest to us, hurt us. And we'll see what causes the glory of the Lord to be revealed the most.

So, recline around the Passover table. Lean with John onto Jesus's breast. Uncover your feet and allow the Lord of the universe to uncake the mud and dust from this world from your soles to between your toes. If you refuse, He says, "You have no part with me."

DAY 28: MORNING
Serve One Another!
(Read John 13:1–11)

The night before His crucifixion, Jesus knew that He was about to die the most grueling of deaths. He knew that He was going to be betrayed, denied and forsaken. Yet, He loved His disciples and wanted to show them how to humbly serve one another and forgive when wronged.

Jesus and the disciples came to what we call the Last Supper. The tables were low to the ground and often times someone's feet were almost even to the level of someone else's face. In the humid climate, the sweat caused the dust of the roads to cling to the feet of those walking in sandals. It was customary for a servant to wash the feet of guests, but there was no servant at the supper.

John records that Jesus washed the feet of the disciples around the time of the meal. In Luke 22:24, after the meal there arose a dispute over who was the greatest. Most likely, Jesus saw the dirty job of cleaning feet as a way to illustrate the need to serve one another. He had earlier taught how to become great in Matthew 20.

Bible scholars have thought that the seating order might have been with John at the right of Jesus (John 13:23), Judas Iscariot at His left (near enough for Jesus to hand him bread, 13:26) and Peter at the lowest end (able to gesture to John across the table, 13:24). Perhaps it was the unexpected seating order that may have led to the discussion of who was the greatest.

Jesus took off His garment, indicating that this was no small job of washing 24 dirty feet. Girded only with a towel around His waist, the Messiah humbly stooped down to wash their feet.

One by one, Jesus, the Master, washed the feet of His disciples, the learners. If you had been one of the disciples, you would have smelled the same stench everyone else smelled. You would have felt the grit between your toes as you walked in the room. You would have seen the caked dust encrusted on the feet of others.

Jesus used this unforgettable opportunity to forever emblazon on the minds of the disciples that in order to be great and the most like the Master, the disciples must serve others.

Pray this prayer to God: *"Dear Jesus: As I read these lessons in the days ahead, help me see the needs of others and be a servant. I know my feet need to be cleansed today but help me as I seek a lowly heart to wash the feet of others. Amen."*

DAY 28: EVENING
Forgive One Another!
(Read John 13:10–17)

In addition to serving one another (this morning's lesson), another lesson can be gleaned from this passage. Three separate words were used: the word *"bathed"* in Greek has a root word from where we get the word "laundry" and "lavatory." Hebrews 10:22 says "having the body *bathed* with pure water" (Young's Literal Translation). *"Wash"* is a different word, usually used for washing parts of the body. As we walk in this sinful earth, our spiritual feet get dirty. Lastly, the word for *"completely clean"* is a word from which we get the word catharsis, which means a cleaning of the digestive system or a purifying inwardly, physically or emotionally. It is the same word used in Matthew 5:8, *"Blessed are the **pure** in heart, for they shall see God."*

To bathe is a symbol of our salvation. To wash symbolizes our need to confess our sins through regular prayer. To be completely clean symbolizes our call for inner purity. The beautiful symbolism here is that God bathes us at salvation, washes us when we do sin, and gives us a purity from within.

What's more, Jesus told the disciples to wash one another's feet. It symbolized their need as well as our need to forgive others. Forgiving others is foundational for the believer. Harboring grudges toward others, especially fellow believers, is unconscionable. God's forgiveness is linked with our forgiving others:

> But if you do not forgive men their trespasses, neither will your Father forgive your trespasses. **Matthew 6:15**

> So My heavenly Father also will do to you if each of you, from his heart, does not forgive his brother his trespasses. **Matthew 18:35**

> And whenever you stand praying, if you have anything against anyone, forgive him, so that your Father in heaven may also forgive you your trespasses. **Mark 11:25**

> Forgive, and you will be forgiven. **Luke 6:37b**

> And if he sins against you seven times in a day, and seven times in a day returns to you, saying, "I repent," you shall forgive him. **Luke 17:4**

> If you forgive the sins of any, they are forgiven them; if you retain the sins of any, they are retained." **John 20:23**

Pray this prayer to God: *"Heavenly Father: Cleanse my feet today. I know when You died on the cross, You bathed me with wholly cleansing water from all my sins. Now, when I fall, wash me and help me to forgive others when they, like me, fall. By Jesus's power I pray. Amen."*

DAY 29: MORNING
When Friends Hurt You
(Read John 13:18–38)

Have you ever been hurt by a friend? By a Christian friend? Have you known churches to argue, fight, even split? If not, be forewarned: If it happened to Jesus, it happens today and will likely happen to you. I have known prominent church leaders who have violated their sacred trust. This devotional is to help prepare you to know how to respond when those closest to you hurt you.

Judas was not an obvious betrayer. He was entrusted with the money of the disciples and seemed genuinely interested in the poor (John 12:4–7; 13:29). When Jesus said a disciple would betray Him, no one pointed to Judas, even when Jesus clearly indicated Judas (John 13:25–30).

God's foreknowledge: The act of betrayal of a friend was especially bad if it was done after eating together. *"Even my own familiar friend in whom I trusted, **who ate my bread,** has lifted up his heel against me"* (Psalm 41:9). This was a prophecy of Judas.

Even though God has foreknowledge, betrayal is not of God (see John 6:70; Luke 22:3; John 13:27). Jesus knew ahead of time what Judas would do (John 6:64) yet chose him anyway. God knows what you are going through.

God's allowance: Years ago, a pastor had a trusted friend, studying for the ministry. The pastor met and prayed daily with the young seminarian. One day, the man kidnapped the pastor's 13-year-old daughter. Even though she was returned, she was traumatized by the assault. When such betrayals of trust occur, we ask, "Where was God?" There are no easy answers to why God allows these things. A church member, pastor, or trusted friend in Christ will likely hurt you to some extent. Unfortunately, it is possible that you too may be an instrument of Satan to hurt someone.

God's understanding: Jesus understands that it is hard to forgive those who hurt us. If there is no repentance in a brother in sin, read 1 Corinthians 5:1–12; Matthew 18:15–17; and 1 Timothy 1:19–20. Resist the desire to return evil for evil and read Romans 12:17–21; Matthew 18:21–35; and James 6:1–2. If there is repentance, read Luke 17:3–5 and 2 Corinthians 2:5–11.

God's sovereignty: If God can use the greatest betrayal in history and turn it into the greatest victory, ask God to give healing and purpose in your hurt. Trust that God will take your grief and to bring glory to Himself in spite of it all.

Pray this prayer to God: *"Jesus, You know how it feels to be betrayed. Comfort me when betrayal comes. I cannot forgive on my own strength, so I ask You to forgive through me. Amen."*

DAY 29: EVENING
Love Revealed In Glory!
(Read John 13:31–14:1)

It seems as out of place as a pit bull at a poodle parlor to see glory attached to the sufferings of the cross. Yet the Bible consistently puts exaltation alongside of degradation. Paul later wrote, *"We glory in tribulation"* (Romans 5:3) and *"I consider that the sufferings of this present time are not worthy to be compared with the glory which shall be revealed in us."* (Romans 8:18). Elsewhere, Paul boldly said *"I take <u>pleasure</u> in infirmities, in reproaches, in needs, in persecutions, in distresses, for Christ's sake. For when I am weak, then I am strong."* (2 Corinthians 12:10, KJV)

Pleasure? Glory in tribulation? If that is so, we might be tempted to say, "Lord, please **don't** show me your glory!" Yet, it is in the furnace that impurities are purged and strength galvanized. Of all the disciples, Peter learned this lesson and later wrote: *⁶In this you greatly rejoice, though now for a little while, if need be, you have been grieved by various trials, ⁷that the genuineness of your faith, being much more precious than gold that perishes, though it is tested by fire, may be found to praise, honor, and glory at the revelation of Jesus Christ.* (1 Peter 1:6–7)

Peter loved Jesus, promised loyalty to death, yet failed Him only hours after his hollow promises. All would eventually abandon Christ that night. Yet, cradled between Judas Iscariot's departure and Peter's foretold denial is the birth of a "new" commandment: *"Love one another as I have loved you."*

How was that commandment new? God commanded people as far back as Deuteronomy 6:5 to love one another. Jesus had already commanded the disciples to love, even their enemies (Matthew 5:44). That love was limited and human, "love your neighbor as yourself." But now, Jesus personified the very heart of the Father's love by demonstrating a new aspect and measure of love: ***"as I have loved you."***

What would happen if Christians truly reflected the love of Jesus? If God demonstrated His love for us while we were still sinners by His giving His life for us (Romans 5:8), then what would be the outcome if we would love each other? According to John 13:35, "By this all will know that you are My disciples, if you have love for one another."

Pray this prayer to God: *"Precious Lord Jesus, I am unworthy to profess my love for You. Forgive me when I fail and deny You, especially when it comes to loving others as You have loved me. Thank You for going to the cross to gain Your glory. Amen."*

—John Chapter 14—

MEMORY VERSE:
"Let not your heart be troubled;
you believe in God, believe also in Me.

(John 14:1)

John, as pastor at Ephesus, surely must have preached his share of funerals. John Chapter 14 is used in times of mourning. John, last of all of the living disciples, likely felt lonely. It wasn't just the disciples he had seen die, but he had heard of thousands of Christians being put to death for the gospel's sake. He had seen the temple burned and destroyed along with countless fellow Jews.

The night before Jesus died, his Lord comforted his disciples with these words. Jesus did not leave them orphans. Though John felt lonely, he was not alone. He had the comfort of the Holy Spirit of Christ living within him.

The sixth "I AM" statement of "I AM the way the truth and the life, no one comes to the Father except through Me" is one of the strongest statements of Christ being the only way to God. It comes after Thomas's question, "Lord, we do not know where You are going, and how can we know the way?" and is linked to the miracle of the nobleman's son (John 4:46–54).

The nobleman believed but insisted twice that Jesus "come down." Jesus said, "Unless you see signs and wonders, you (plural) will not believe." Like the nobleman, Thomas would later learn that believing is not always seeing.

DAY 30: MORNING
Love Revealed Through Faith!
(John 14:1–6)

Someone asked me on Facebook what I would tell my younger self if I could. I said, "Don't sweat the small stuff." Jesus was about to leave this world and told the disciples, "Don't sweat the **big** stuff." Well, not exactly in those words, but He told them there were hard times ahead. Then He says, "Don't let your heart be troubled." And just how are we supposed to do that? Typical of Jesus, He tells us how in John 14.

Peace of Christ *"Let not your heart be troubled."* Jesus said this as He was soon to be crucified. You too can have peace.

Place of Faith *"you believe in God, believe also in Me."* What are you trusting in? Finances, friends, abilities, power? Seek God's kingdom first, putting your faith in Him.

Personal Place *"In My Father's house"* Heaven is not on a cloud or a quiet boring place. Jesus related it to a personal, family home, where you can find rest and peace.

Plentiful Place *"are many mansions"* Do you think there may not be room for you? Jesus has prepared a large, plentiful place for those who trust Him (see Revelation 7:9).

Promised Place *"if it were not so, I would have told you."* People may be dishonest, but you can trust Jesus. He not only told the truth, He is the truth.

Prepared by Christ *"I go to prepare a place for you."* Our place in Heaven is not a cookie cutter house; it is prepared uniquely for you, custom-built by Christ Himself.

Preceded by Christ *"I will come again and receive you to Myself."* Isn't it good to follow a guide who has already been there? Jesus will personally come and take us there.

Presence of Christ *"where I am, there you may be also."* Some translations call the "mansions" as "dwelling places" or "apartments." I don't care as long as Jesus is there.

Passage provided *"where I go you know, and the way you know."* This is not a hope so, think so, maybe so. We can know where we are going and how to get there.

Perplexing questions *"Lord, we do not know where You are going, and how can we know the way?"* Do you have questions? That is okay. We know He has the answers.

Powerful answer *"I am the way, the truth, and the life."* Drop the microphone.

Provision by Christ *"No one comes to the Father except through Me."* Don't trust in people, or other faiths or even yourself. Trust only in the work of Christ on the cross.

By keeping these heavenly perspectives, we can remember that even the big stuff is small stuff for Him. Just remember, Jesus sees the big picture.

Pray this prayer to God: *"Jesus, thank You for being the Way, the Truth and the Life. Give me a heavenly perception so that nothing would trouble my heart. Amen."*

DAY 30: EVENING
Love Revealed Through Jesus Christ
(Read John 14:7–14)

This morning we saw that love was revealed through faith. But faith alone is not enough. Love and faith must be placed in a trustworthy person. In chapters 13, 14, and 15, the word "love" is mentioned more than 20 times, more than anywhere else in three consecutive chapters of the gospels.

When Jesus says, *"Let not your heart be troubled,"* He is speaking to His disciples, but He is also speaking to us today. The best way to keep our hearts from being troubled is to know the love of Christ.

It is innate within all of us to have a "troubled heart" at times. Even Jesus was on occasions "troubled" in His soul (John 12:27) and in His spirit (John 13:21). Because of this tendency within all of us, Jesus commands us to strive for our hearts to not be troubled nor afraid (notice He repeats this phrase again in John 14:27).

How can we keep our hearts from being stirred up, anxious, disquieted, and not at peace? The antidote is found in 14:1: Belief/Faith/Trust.

Belief, faith, and trust all mean that we have to put our confidence in Someone else (Jesus and His Father), rather than ourselves. "Trust God…and Me." Jesus commands us to trust Him in verses 1, 10, 11, 12, 13, and 14. We trust that Jesus went to His Father's house, is preparing a place for us, will come again to take us there, and is the only way to get there.

Kyle Idleman wrote a book entitled *Gods At War*, with its title meaning that there are many gods who are at war to take your attention away from the true God. One of the chief false gods in this world is the god named Worry.

The third disciple Jesus called was Phillip (John 1:43), yet still he did not understand that Jesus Christ was the bodily manifestation of the Heavenly Father. Even though he and the rest of the disciples had been personally taught by Jesus Christ Himself over the past three and a half years, Phillip and Thomas still had questions.

When we have questions, the answer ultimately will be to believe (verse 11). It is not to be sincere or do your best. The answer is to believe that Jesus is the only way to get to God the Father. Jesus is not "a way" but "THE way."

Pray this prayer to God: *"Heavenly Father, thank You for revealing yourself to us through Jesus Christ. Help me to trust You and Your love for me more. Thank You that whatever I pray in Your Name, according to Your will, You will do. Amen."*

DAY 31: MORNING
Love Revealed In Obedience
(Read John 14:15–24)

Have you truly and completely trusted Jesus Christ as your Lord and Savior? If you trust Him with the salvation of your eternal life, which is far greater than anything in this temporal world, should you not also trust Him by obeying Him in your actions while you are here on earth? In other words, if you truly trust Him, you will obey Him.

There is a problem we all have with people who say with their mouths that they have trusted Jesus for salvation, and yet they do not keep His commandments. (John 14:15, 21, and 24).

James, the half-brother of Jesus, did not believe in Jesus as Savior until after His resurrection. Later, however, he would write that "faith without works is dead," meaning that a person is not truly a Christian who only professes faith but has no actions to back it up. Believers are proven to be righteous not only by what they say they believe but also how their life is lived as a result of their faith (James 2:24).

The love relationship between God and His children is not a one-time profession with no change in behavior. You don't simply pray a prayer, and everything is all finished! True love is shown by how we are changed. We do not change our ways and obey God's commands to receive God's love. Our response to God's love is to first love Him back.

> *"This is love, not that we love God, but that He loved us and sent His Son to be an atoning sacrifice for our sins...We love Him because He first loved us."* (1 John 4:10, 19).

If we have truly received the God of the universe into our lives, we have received the very essence and manifestation of God (John 14:21, 23–24). With that essence within us, we cannot help but follow in obedience. That is the proof that we truly love God.

Can you explain that God the Father, God the Son, and the Holy Spirit of Truth all three will dwell in your life? (See John 14:17, 21, 23).

We as Christians aren't the only ones who reveal our love in obedience. Look at John 14:31. Jesus doesn't ask us to do anything He hasn't already done. Jesus demonstrated His love for His Father in His obedience, *"as the Father gave Me commandment, so I do."*

Pray this prayer to God: *"Dear God, I confess I have received You into my life. You are my Lord and God, not just for my eternal salvation, but also for my life here on earth. Help me keep your commandments in my life. In Jesus's name. Amen."*

DAY 31: EVENING
Love Revealed In The Holy Spirit
(Read John 14: 25–26)

For two days now we have been discovering how love is revealed to us and in us. When you receive God the Father into your life, you receive God's Holy Spirit. When you receive Jesus Christ into your life, you receive the Spirit of Christ.

Love is revealed in us through the Holy Spirit, God's Spirit, and Christ's Spirit.

⁹But you are not in the flesh but in the Spirit, if indeed <u>the Spirit of God dwells in you.</u> Now if anyone does not <u>have the Spirit of Christ, he is not His.</u> ¹⁰And if Christ is in you, the body is dead because of sin, but the Spirit is life because of righteousness. ¹¹But if the <u>Spirit of Him who raised Jesus from the dead dwells in you,</u> He who raised Christ from the dead will also give life to your mortal bodies through His Spirit who dwells in you.   **Romans 8:9–11**

Paul later reveals that having *"Christ in you, the hope of all glory,"* was a mystery throughout the Old Testament and is revealed in the New Testament through the Holy Spirit (See Colossians 1:26–28).

Jesus in John 14 calls God's Spirit in us the "Comforter" or "Helper," and is also translated as "Advocate." John later uses that same word "Advocate" in describing Jesus in Heaven. It is as though that God's Holy Spirit is doing the same thing for us on earth (Helping, Comforting, Advocating) that Jesus is doing at the right hand of the Father.

The Holy Spirit is the Spirit of Truth, and accomplishes the following things:

1) **Abides in us forever**
2) **Cannot be received by the world**
3) **Teaches us all things, bringing to our remembrance Jesus's words**
4) **Is better for the Spirit to dwell in us than for Christ to be here on earth**
5) **Convicts of sin, righteousness, and judgment**
6) **Guides us and speaks to us into all truth**
7) **Glorifies Jesus Christ by declaring things from Christ**

Being a Christian is more than saying a prayer, agreeing with Biblical truth and having a good answer to God's question of why He should let you into heaven. It is having the living Christ dwelling in you.

Pray this prayer to God: *"Spirit of the Living God, fall fresh on me. As I have received Your Spirit, teach me to walk in the Spirit, live in the Spirit and worship in the Spirit. In Jesus's Name. Amen."*

DAY 32: MORNING
What Can The Holy Spirit Do For You?
(Read John 14:26–27)

I have shared with children that if you make a home in your heart for God, He will make a home in His heaven for you when this life on earth is over. Like a child who hosts a sleepover or a birthday party at his house, and then later gets to go spend some time with his friends, Jesus promises His Spirit will stay with the believers and equally promises He will come back for them to bring them to His Father's house.

When we are saved, we are baptized in the Holy Spirit. When we are controlled by God, we are filled with the Holy Spirit. The Holy Spirit is our Helper. But perhaps the greatest thing about the Holy Spirit is that He is at home in our hearts.

Jesus is trying to give peace to His disciples by telling them of all of the good things He is going to prepare in heaven, while still giving reassurance that until He comes to bring them home, they will not be left as orphans. Both the Father and the Son will come and make their home within the believers. How? Through the Holy Spirit. As you grow, ask the Holy Spirit to teach you all things and to also keep them in your "remembrance" (verse 26).

This passage here teaches one of the most profound and hardest to understand truths in Scripture: The Trinity. We as Christians believe in one God, but He is manifest in three personages: The Father, Son, and Holy Spirit. When Christ lives in you, that entity inside you is the Holy Spirit.

However, just because we have the Spirit, and just because the Spirit will help us and teach us, all of those things will not mean we will understand everything. In those times, Jesus promises us peace, but not externally in the world, but internally in the heart.

Jesus promises peace, but He does not promise peace from the things in this world. In fact, we will not feel like we are at home until He returns for us. The ruler of this world at this time is not Jesus, nor His Father, but of course the great Satan, to whom God has temporarily given partial control of the world. When humanity fell, God purposely let the devil rule here on earth temporarily as a consequence for our sins. (We will see more of this in the next devotional and in John 17).

But even so, God is still in ultimate charge. And He gives us His Holy Spirit to make a little Heaven for us on earth.

Pray this prayer to God: *"Lord, there are things I just do not understand. There are things that happen that just don't make sense. In those times, let me long for Your return for me to take me home. Let me never get used to being here. In Jesus's Name. Amen."*

DAY 32: EVENING
We Are Not At Home In This World
(Read John 14:28–31)

Do you feel a little uneasy in the world? Are you longing for something, but you can't quite put your finger on it? Don't worry and don't fear. Jesus is coming back to take us to a home that we have never been to before.

How can it be home if we've never been there? Because our Father, our Savior and our spiritual family of brothers and sisters are there. Jesus said to the disciples that they should rejoice that He was going back to the Father (John 14:28). I understand how the disciples felt. I have been to many a funeral and while I know my loved ones are now in heaven with our Savior and loved ones, I know I am going to miss them and to be honest I don't always feel like rejoicing at a funeral.

And that is okay. Jesus, as you may recall, wept at Lazarus's funeral. It is not a sign of lack of faith or even a sign of lack of joy for them. It is a sign of our love on how much we will miss those who have gone on to glory.

But I also think that sadness at a funeral is a sign that we are not at home in this world. If death is so natural, if dying is a part of life (the last part, that is), then why don't we shrug our shoulders and move on.

> **Ecclesiastes 3:11**
>
> Even though death is inevitable, there is a reason that it is still unwelcomed. We were created to be eternal beings and God has place eternity in our hearts.

The Father is greater than we are, and He really does know best. When death comes to pass, whether it was the death of Jesus as foretold in John 14:29, or in our own lives when loved ones die, we can mourn and miss the departed. When the cruelty of this world and its ruler, Satan, seems to have solidly taken charge of this earth, we can say with Jesus, "He has nothing in me." Why? Because, as the old saying goes, "the world didn't give it to me and the world can't take it away."

Maybe Jesus said it better with His words in Matthew 6:20. *"But lay up for yourselves treasures in heaven, where neither moth nor rust destroys and where thieves do not break in and steal."*

Makes you a little home-sick, doesn't it?

Pray this prayer to God: *"Dear God in Heaven, my heart and my spirit are with You, hidden in Christ's heart at Your right hand. Help me to have a heavenly perspective on this world. When I get weary by the world's wicked ways, let me remember this is not my home. In Jesus's Name. Amen."*

—John Chapter 15—

MEMORY VERSE:
Greater love has no one than this,
than to lay down one's life for his friends.

(John 15:13)

The Passover meal was over. Four cups of wine had been poured and consumed (three by our Lord, saving the last for when He returns for us). The closing hymn of the Passover had been sung. Their feet had been washed, only to return again to the night air and the walk across the Kidron Valley to the Garden of Gethsemane. As they walked, they saw the grapevines beneath the full moon.

John's mind ached as much as his hand did from writing, reaching for yet another memory to be brought to his thoughts and to his fingers to share with those who would read his final gospel.

There it is, the memory with such vivid detail, it had to be inspired by the Holy Spirit. Lessons he had preached on for years were now finally being put down with paper, pen, and ink for generations to come.

Lessons on fruit and pruning. Oh, he knew about pruning! Lessons on being chosen by Christ, lessons on the world and its staining sin. Lessons on the Holy Spirit, the "Holy Advocate," John loved to say.

But most of all, John recalled the most recurring lesson. It was the lesson that Jesus most taught and, even more, the lesson that Jesus most readily lived. The lesson and the life of Jesus was love. *No one had loved John the way Jesus did, not even his mother Salome, or even Jesus's mother Mary, though she greatly adored John's care of her in her dying years.*

John knew Jesus did not love him more than the other disciples. But this was John's gospel, John's story. And if he wanted to call himself the "disciple whom Jesus loved," he would. No, Jesus didn't love John more than the others, but Jesus did love John more than any other.

John closed his eyes.

"This is My commandment, that you love one another as I have loved you. Greater love has no one than this, than to lay down one's life for his friends."

The aged disciple opened his tired eyes now moistened by the almost audible memory of His Lord's voice, dabbed his tear-stained face with his shirt sleeve and picked up his pen…

DAY 33: MORNING
No Fruit, Fruit, More Fruit, Much Fruit
(Read John 15:1–8)

God often referred to Israel as a vine. Jesus said that He is "The True Vine." God the Father takes care of the vine, the branches, the fruit, and the fruitless branches.

No fruit. There are two that do not bear fruit. The first are fruitless branches in Christ which are taken away. It literally means God "takes up" or "picks up" (the same word is used in John 5:8 and 8:59). If you are not bearing fruit, God notices and He will "lift you up" out of the dirt to help you bear fruit.

There are those who are fruitless but not abiding in Christ (verse 6). They are cast out *as* branches, withered and burned, but they are not Christians. Read from Hebrews 12:

6For the Lord disciplines him whom He loves and chastises every son whom He receives." 7It is for discipline that you have to endure. God is treating you as sons; for what son is there whom his father does not discipline? 8If you are left without discipline, in which all have participated, then you are illegitimate children and not sons… 11For the moment all discipline seems painful rather than pleasant; later it yields the peaceful fruit of righteousness to those who have been trained by it.

Fruit and more fruit. If you bear fruit (15:2), Jesus said God will prune you to bear more fruit. The word "prune" is the same as "clean" in John 13:10. The Father will purge you (purify) to produce more fruit.

Much fruit. To bear much fruit, you must abide in Christ (15:5). When we keep His words *in* us, His desires are met in our desires. He is glorified in our bearing fruit.

Remaining fruit. Physical vines produce temporal fruit, but Christian fruit remains (John 15:16). Christ remains in you forever (John 14:16), and His fruit abides forever.

> *43For a good tree does not bear bad fruit, nor does a bad tree bear good fruit. 45A good man out of the good treasure of his heart brings forth good; and an evil man out of the evil treasure of his heart brings forth evil.* **(Luke 6:43–45)**

> *22But the fruit of the Spirit is love, joy, peace, longsuffering, kindness, goodness, faithfulness, 23gentleness, self-control. Against such there is no law.* **(Galatians 5:22–23)**

> *13I often planned to come to you (but was hindered until now), that I might have some fruit among you also, just as among the other Gentiles.* **(Romans 1:13)**

Pray this prayer to God: *"Precious Lord Jesus, I confess there are times when I am fruitless. I do not always act like a Christian, I sometimes do not feel like a Christian, and I certainly do not lead others to become Christians as much as I should. I commit to abide in and obey Your word so that I can bear much fruit. Amen."*

DAY 33: EVENING
Love: The Source Of Fruit
(Read John 15:9–17)

When the Apostle Paul wrote about the fruit of the Spirit in Galatians 5, he did not say "The fruits of the Spirit are…" He said "The fruit of the Spirit is love…" listing other attributes of the fruit of the Spirit. All of the descriptions (joy, peace, longsuffering, kindness, goodness, faithfulness, gentleness, self-control) were attributes of THE fruit of love.

Without love, everything else is meaningless. See 1 Corinthians 13, the "love chapter" (The Message):

¹If I speak with human eloquence and angelic ecstasy but don't love, I'm nothing but the creaking of a rusty gate. ²If I speak God's Word with power, revealing all his mysteries and making everything plain as day, and if I have faith that says to a mountain, "Jump," and it jumps, but I don't love, I'm nothing. ³If I give everything I own to the poor and even go to the stake to be burned as a martyr, but I don't love, I've gotten nowhere. So, no matter what I say, what I believe, and what I do, I'm bankrupt without love. ⁴Love never gives up. Love cares more for others than for self. Love doesn't want what it doesn't have. Love doesn't strut, doesn't have a swelled head, ⁵doesn't force itself on others, isn't always "me first," doesn't fly off the handle, doesn't keep score of the sins of others, ⁶doesn't revel when others grovel, takes pleasure in the flowering of truth, ⁷puts up with anything, trusts God always, always looks for the best, never looks back, but keeps going to the end. ⁸Love never dies. Inspired speech will be over some day; praying in tongues will end; understanding will reach its limit…¹³But for right now, until that completeness, we have three things to do to lead us toward that consummation: Trust steadily in God, hope unswervingly, love extravagantly. And the best of the three is love.

Love is not a nice warm feeling. Love is not the icing on the Christian cake. Love is the flour, the sugar, the egg, the mixing bowl, the spoon, and the oven it is made in. Finishing that analogy, love is only completed when the fire of unloving people, unlovely circumstances, and unloving feelings come. When those testing times come, remember: Without love, God would not have sent Jesus (John 3:16).

Without love, Jesus wouldn't have laid down His life (Romans 5:8). Without love, God would not have chosen us before the foundation of the world (Ephesians 1:4). Without love, we would be separated from God and Christ (Romans 8:39). How dare we say we love God if we don't love others?

Pray this prayer to God: *"Abba, Daddy, sometimes I forget You are my loving Daddy. I take for granted Your love. If You love all of us, despite our sins, surely, I can love others. I really mean it when I say this: I love You. Amen."*

DAY 34: MORNING
Who Chose Whom?
(Read John 15:16)

Tucked away in today's verse is a truth that confounds many a theologian and frustrates many a seeker: If God chose some, does He not choose others? Jesus said, *"You did not choose Me, but I chose you and appointed you..."*

In the 500 words or less devotional below, I cannot answer this question adequately (that is my cop-out and I am sticking with it). But, if you are a Christian and have chosen Christ, remember that God chose you first. When He created you, He put a soft, sensitive spot in your heart, and combined that heart with the environment He also created especially for only you. As a result, within your own free will, you turned to Him in trust for your salvation and chose Him, after He chose you.

It is awesome to ponder that God saw and chose you. You matter to Him. He chose you for His purpose and His pleasure. Rick Warren writes, "The moment you were born into the world, God was there as an unseen witness, smiling at your birth...You are a child of God, and you bring pleasure to God like nothing else he has ever created. The Bible says, 'Because of his love God had already decided that through Jesus Christ he would make us his children—this was his pleasure and purpose.'"[1]

We may not understand how God chose us in salvation without conflicting with our free will, yet He did (Ephesians 1:4). The name "church" means "called out ones, the elect." Even greater is that He is not finished with us. Read Romans 8:29–30

[29]For whom He <u>foreknew</u>, He also <u>predestined to be conformed to the image of His Son</u>, that He might be the firstborn among many brethren. [30]Moreover whom He predestined, these He also called; whom He called, these He also justified; and whom He justified, these He also glorified.

Your birth was God's design, but so was your salvation. If it seems too awesome to ponder the question of "Why me?" look to Him for the answer: "Because He is God and He does as He wills." And He chose you. I partially quoted John 15:16 in the first paragraph. It ends with Jesus saying that He *"appointed you to go and bear fruit--fruit that will last. Then the Father will give you whatever you ask in My name."*

Pray this prayer to God: *"Oh, Lord my God, when I in awesome wonder, consider all the worlds Thy hands have made, then shall I bow in humble adoration, and there proclaim: My God, how great Thou art! Thank You for choosing me and allowing me to choose You. In Jesus's Name. Amen."*

---

1   Rick Warren, *The Purpose Driven Life* (Zondervan: Grand Rapids), pg. 63. The Biblical reference is Ephesians 1:5 (Today's English Version—Good News Translation)

Can people be so cruel as to kill the only begotten Son of God? The answer is sadly yes and the world would do it again if it had the chance. The closest thing the world can do now is hate those who are in Christ; that is, the church. We believers have the Holy Spirit of Christ and represent Jesus Christ to the world until He returns.

Read verses 22 and 24. The phrase "they would have no sin" if Jesus had not come does not mean that everyone would have been perfect, or all would have gone to heaven, or even have an excuse to sin out of ignorance.

The passage seems to say that people would not have been held accountable for their sins, but it really says the opposite. If Jesus hadn't come, they would not have been guilty of the greatest sin: the open hatred and rejection of the love of Jesus Christ. Instead they would have only their sins. There were murders, robberies, thefts, adulteries, and millions of other sins before Jesus came. People would have been (and still are) guilty of those things, and they would have (and still will) face judgment for them.

But to reject God's only Son and to reject God's love is to say in effect, "We hate You, God!" That is the sin they would not have on their account. And that is the greatest sin of all. Every person who rejects Christ will be held accountable for the sin of hatred of God. They will be held accountable for one sin: The rejection of His freely-offered salvation and forgiveness given totally by grace, available to all who believe. Without His coming, there would be no possibility for their atonement for their many sins.

Sometimes we get judgmental about other people's sins, as if their sins are greater than ours. But 1 Corinthians 6 puts it this way, **"⁹Do you not know that the unrighteous will not inherit the kingdom of God? Do not be deceived. Neither fornicators, nor idolaters, nor adulterers, nor homosexuals, nor sodomites, ¹⁰nor thieves, nor covetous, nor drunkards, nor revilers, nor extortioners will inherit the kingdom of God."**

Whew, that is a pretty sorry lot, right? Paul goes on to say, **"¹¹And such were some of you. But you were washed, but you were sanctified, but you were justified in the name of the Lord Jesus and by the Spirit of our God."**

Pray this prayer to God: *"I love You Lord, and I lift my voice to worship You, O my soul rejoice. Take joy my King in what You hear. May it be a sweet, sweet sound in Your ear. In Jesus's Name. Amen."*

—John Chapter 16—

MEMORY VERSE:

These things I have spoken to you, that in Me you may have peace. In the world you will have tribulation; but be of good cheer, I have overcome the world."

(John 16:33)

In chapter 16, Jesus concludes His final teachings and touches on all of these things. He primarily focuses on His "going" and the Holy Spirit's "coming."

This is a good time to remember why Jesus came in the first place and why John wrote this gospel: *"but these are written that you may believe that Jesus is the Christ, the Son of God, and that believing you may have life in His name."* (John 20:31)

Jesus strikes a recurring theme: this world has trouble, but He has overcome the world. The last 2,000 years of history has shown that Jews persecuted the Christians in the name of religion, then the Romans persecuted the Christians in the name of religion, then Muslims persecuted the Christians, and Christians persecuted the Muslims, Catholics persecuted the Protestants, and then Protestants persecuted other Protestants. Now in the 21st century, what dominates the news? Persecution by those who think they are doing God's work.

The solution is found in Christ, that our joy is found in Him and not in the world.

DAY 35: MORNING
"I go away"
(Read John 16:1–6, 16–28)

For months, Jesus had talked about going away, and now His hour had come. John 16:5 says, *"Now…none of you asks Me, 'Where are you going?'"* They had stopped asking because they finally understood He was speaking of His death. Review some passages where Jesus had talked about His departure:

> Jesus therefore said, *"For a little while longer I am with you, then I go to Him who sent Me.* **John 7:33**

> *"I go away…where I am going, you cannot come."* Therefore the Jews were saying, *"Surely He will not kill Himself, will He…?"* **John 8:21–22**

> *"Little children, I am with you a little while longer. You shall seek Me; and as I said to the Jews, I now say to you also, 'Where I am going, you cannot come.'* **John 13:33**

> *"And where I go you know, and the way you know."* Thomas said to Him, *"Lord, we do not know where You are going, and how can we know the way?"* **John 14:5, 6**

> *"You heard Me say to you, 'I go away, and I will come to you.' If you loved Me, you would have rejoiced, because I go to the Father; for the Father is greater than I."* **John 14:28**

The disciples who had listened to statements like these for years finally realized He was not speaking figuratively. He was not going to the Gentiles. He was not going to usher in His kingdom by force. He was going to die. As that truth sank in, sorrow filled their hearts (16:6).

The disciples were confused with Jesus's *"a little while…"* statements (16:17). All they knew was that weeks earlier, they had seen Jesus raise a dead man from the grave and only days prior, throngs of people had ushered Jesus into Jerusalem like a King! Seeing their confusion, Jesus plainly told them that their sorrow will turn to joy (16:20).

There will be times as a Christian in which you will be confused and question God. John 16:19 says, *"Jesus knew they desired to ask Him…"* Ask God to clear it up for you. Study the Bible. Listen to sermons. Make sure the answers are based on the Bible. If you can't find answers based on God's Word, keep asking until someone can give you a solidly Biblical answer.

Pray this prayer to God: *"Jesus, I come to You with my problems, my questions, my confusion and my sorrow. Thank You that You are with me always. Help me make it through all my 'little while' times. Amen."*

DAY 35: EVENING
The Holy Spirit Revealed In The Godhead
(Read John 16:7–15)

In the section "Love revealed in the Holy Spirit" (Day 31: Evening), we saw seven things the Holy Spirit *does*. The following is an overview of who the Holy Spirit *is*.

The Spirit is God. The Holy Spirit is a Person in the Triune Godhead: thoroughly unified as God, but three separate and distinct manifestations. The one true God relates with His creation in three expressions, as Father, as Son, and as Holy Spirit.

God the Father is above and beyond all things and is invisible and unseen by humans (*No one has seen God at any time. The only begotten Son, who is in the bosom of the Father, He has declared Him,* John 1:18). When God is "seen" by humanity, it is not God in totality but only a manifestation of the unseen infinite God.

God the Son is the expression of God physically (*He [Jesus] is the image of the invisible God, the firstborn over all creation* Colossians 1:15; *God … has in these last days spoken to us by His Son … who being the brightness of His glory and the express image of His person…purged our sins* Hebrews 1:1–3). The Holy Spirit has always existed (*… Christ Jesus, who, being in the form of God, did not consider it robbery to be equal with God, but made Himself of no reputation, taking the form of a bondservant, and coming in the likeness of men* Philippians 2:5–7).

God the Holy Spirit relates to us spiritually. He is the same Spirit within the Father and the Son (*And if Christ is in you, … the Spirit is life because of righteousness. But if the Spirit of Him who raised Jesus from the dead dwells in you, He … will also give life to your mortal bodies through His Spirit who dwells in you* **Romans 8:10–11**).

The Holy Spirit has always existed (*How much more shall the blood of Christ, who through the eternal Spirit offered Himself without spot to God, cleanse your conscience from dead works to serve the living God?* **Hebrews 9:14**). He is in all believers permanently (*And I will pray the Father, and He will give you another Helper, that He may abide with you forever…If anyone loves Me, he will keep My word; and My Father will love him, and We will come to him and make Our home with him* **John 14:16, 23**)

God's Holy Spirit interacts with non-believers (**John 16:9**), with the Father and Son (**John 16:10**) and with Satan (**John 16:11**). The Holy Spirit is a Person. Jesus says "*I will send Him*" (**16:7**). He does not say, "I will send It."

Pray this prayer to God: "*Spirit of the Living God, fall fresh on me. I want to be so saturated and immersed in Your Spirit that we walk as one. In the Name of Him who sent the Spirit into all believers I pray. Amen.*"

DAY 36: MORNING
We May Be Lonely...
(Assorted passages, based on John 16:6–15)

The Holy Spirit baptizes believers at salvation. Baptism in the Holy Spirit is an immersion of the Holy Spirit within us (*for John truly baptized with water, but you shall be baptized with the Holy Spirit not many days from now* **Acts 1:5**). It occurs at salvation when we ask God to cleanse us by the resurrection of Christ (*Corresponding to that, baptism now saves you--not the removal of dirt from the flesh, but an appeal to God for a good conscience--through the resurrection of Jesus Christ* 1 Peter 3:21, NASB).

He gives assurance of our salvation. (*The Spirit Himself bears witness with our spirit that we are children of God* Romans 8:16).

He seals believers until our redemption. (*And do not grieve the Holy Spirit of God, by whom you were sealed for the day of redemption.* Ephesians 4:30--see 2 Corinthians 1:22; Ephesians 1:13).

He fills believers. When we submit to God, the Holy Spirit manifests Himself. We are commanded to be filled with the Spirit (Ephesians 5:18), so it is an act of obedience. Not all believers are "full of the Holy Spirit." (*"Therefore, brethren, seek out from among you seven men of good reputation, full of the Holy Spirit and wisdom, whom we may appoint over this business."* Acts 6:3)

He lives in believers. God's Spirit personally resides in believers. (*Do you not know that you are the temple of God and that the Spirit of God dwells in you?* 1 Corinthians 3:16) We are possessed by the Spirit. (*Or do you not know that your body is the temple of the Holy Spirit who is in you, whom you have from God, and you are not your own?* 1 Corinthians 6:19)

He gives spiritual gifts. Romans 12, 1 Corinthians 12, Ephesians 4, and 1 Peter 4 describe "spiritual gifts," which build up believers (*But the manifestation of the Spirit is given to each one for the profit of all.* 1 Corinthians 12:7. *Since you are zealous for spiritual gifts, let it be for the edification of the church.* 1 Corinthians 14:12)

He imparts spiritual fruit. Galatians 5:22–23 lists the fruit of the Holy Spirit.

He teaches believers. The Spirit teaches us (Luke 12:12; John 14:26), not by human wisdom (1 Corinthians 2:13). Teaching is a gift of the Holy Spirit (1 Corinthians 12:28).

He empowers believers. Jesus said the Holy Spirit will impart power on the disciples (Luke 24:49; Acts 1:8).

Pray this prayer to God: *"Make me a witness, Heavenly Father, and not only a witness but a good witness of what You have done for me. Help me to tell others of Your saving love for us. As You sent Jesus, so send me. Amen."*

Day 36: Evening
... With God's Holy Spirit, We Are Never Alone
(Read John 16:23–33)

There is so much more to say about the Holy Spirit, but many a preacher would be wise to learn the lesson from Christ Himself, who said, *"I still have many things to say to you, but you cannot bear them now."* (John 16:12)

Jesus said one day, the disciples will no longer ask Him questions, and all God's people said, "What a day that will be!" Until then, we can ask questions of Christ, we can ask in the name of Jesus, and we will receive so that our joy will be full.

Questions are not doubts, but rather questions are ways that we learn more about God. If you have ever met an inquisitive child, you can bet your bottom dollar that child is intelligent. If you are a part of the "we've got questions" club, rest assured that you are not the first who has pondered any particular question and somewhere in the history of Christianity, your question has been answered. The answer may not be to a skeptic's satisfaction, but that is what theology and Biblical scholarship is all about.

In fact, there is an entire field of study called "apologetics" which comes from the Greek word which means "defense." 1 Pet. 3:15 says, *"But sanctify the Lord God in your hearts, and always be ready to give a defense to everyone who asks you a reason for the hope that is in you...."*

I taught a class on apologetics for a year to high school students. I now regularly lead groups to a conference, cleverly called an [un]apologetics conference. We are unapologetic in our faith, but we are ready to defend it. There are apologetic Bibles, books, and resources which reaffirm that we do not have to commit "intellectual suicide" in order to believe in God.

But the best defense we have for our faith may not convince a single person but it reassures me more than any argument. It is summed up in a hymn, "You ask me how I know He lives, He lives within my heart."

As Jesus concludes, the disciples think they understand what the Master is saying (29–30). Jesus questions them about whether they now believe, predicting that all would leave Him, except for His Heavenly Father. There are times as believers we may be lonely, but we are never alone. God is with us. He will never leave us or forsake us (Hebrews 13:5).

Pray this prayer to God: *"Thank You God for Your Holy Spirit that dwells permanently in me. Help me to understand You as Father, Son, and Holy Spirit. Give me peace in my tribulations. Thank You that no matter what, I am never alone. Amen."*

—John Chapter 17—

MEMORY VERSE:
*And this is eternal life, that they may know You, the only true God,
and Jesus Christ whom You have sent.*

(John 17:3)

Peter tightened his outer garment against the crisp spring breeze as they walked under the glow of the gloriously full moon, their pathway bathed with soothing light. The chill reminded him that the last vestiges of winter were ebbing away. Buds of life were now returning to the high arid lands of Jerusalem.

Gethsemane lay just ahead but since he was not sure where they were heading, Peter and the disciples let the Master lead. The Rabbi's steps were slower than his usual stringent, decisive pace. Jesus was unlike any other man Peter had ever known. Months earlier, Peter had boldly proclaimed that Jesus was indeed the Messiah, the anointed one, for whom Israel had waited so long. Yet this Nazarene was an enigma.

All of the disciples were weary from the late night they had the evening before, asking Jesus about the coming of the Kingdom. Tonight, Passover's four cups of wine made Peter even sleepier. "Maybe soon we'll bed down early for the night," the fisherman thought.

Finally, Jesus told eight of the disciples to stop and sit and then motioned for Peter, James, and John to follow him a little further. The three glanced at each other's dimly lit faces. Miracles especially happened when the four of them were together. Peter's weariness did not stop his pulse from suddenly pounding.

Without turning around, Jesus's hand went up. "Wait here, as I go and pray there." As he lowered his hand, his head also sank. He slowly went to a small clearing amidst the olive and sycamore trees, not more than a stone's throw away. There he knelt. There he fell on his face. There he prayed.

Peter knew how long his Master prayed. "This might take a while," Simon thought, trying to sit comfortably, his back against a tree as he waited, just as Jesus had instructed. The Rabbi's words faintly wafted over the cool air, sifting with the wind through the branches of the garden trees. Peter's bleary eyes peered through the dark to see the full moon break through the freshly-formed clouds to shine on Jesus. His face was taut and grimacing with troubled eyes lifted upward to his unseen Father with a passion even Peter had not seen before.

Peter also prayed, but not with such boldness to lift his eyes upwards. He glanced at the young brothers, James and his kid brother John. "Humph. Dozing already. Sons of thunder indeed…by snoring!" he thought. Peter echoed the words he had heard from the Master. "Abba, Father, all things are possible for You. Take this cup away from Me; nevertheless, not what I will, but what You will…" The Rock closed his eyes to concentrate on his praying.

Suddenly the voice was closer. "SIMON, are you sleeping?" Peter's eyes jolted open to see His Lord, no longer kneeling, but standing in front of the three disciples. His piercing eyes were not judging but tenderly sad. "Could you not watch one hour? Watch and pray, or else you will fall into temptation. I know your spirits are willing, but your flesh is weak."

Peter watched Him return to the clearing and locked sheepish gazes with the two brothers. "Had it been an hour already?" This time, Peter sank to the ground on his knees and elbows with the name "Simon" ringing in his ears. He had been called Simon all of his life, especially by his father Jonas as they fished and cleaned their nets, by his brother when he came running breathlessly with a tale so fantastic. He immediately thought his fanatical young brother had gone completely off the deep end.

"Simon, we have found the Christ," Andrew had proclaimed four years earlier, as he ran up to Peter, alongside of John. Simon, not at all a religious man like his brother, was not convinced. First, Andrew was following that "crazy John the Baptizer" who was practically drowning people in the dirty Jordan River, Simon thought. Now his kid brother and little John were convinced that a Nazarene was the Anointed One. A Nazarene? They were just looking for a way to ditch fishing, leaving Simon and James to do all the heavy work. But when this man Jesus, if he was merely a man, called him "Peter," his heart quivered. His impulsive brashness turned to a deeper boldness. He never wanted to be called Simon again.

His memories of the last three years distracted him from praying. It wasn't just his name that changed, *he* had changed. He shifted his knees and tried praying in a less dignified position, now his belly on the cold ground, but elbows still up. Hearing Jesus call him Simon made his face flush with embarrassment. He loved the name Peter, the Rock, solid, dependable, not shifting. Not Simon.

His knees felt better but now it was his elbows that ached. He shifted again. He couldn't concentrate. Simon suddenly realized he wasn't praying. "It's not like I'm not laying down, I am prostrating myself before the Lord…" he thought, getting off his achy elbows and fully putting his weight on his belly, chest and legs. "…just like the prophets prayed."

Face to the ground, his thoughts wandered back to the meal. "Is it I?" he asked his Master, following the statement Jesus had made that one of the disciples was going to betray him. Jesus answered Simon with something that surely was another one of his mysterious parables.

"Deny you? I WILL NEVER DENY YOU," Simon proclaimed as accusing eyes gazed at him around the table. "They'll deny you, but I won't. Jesus, please."

The only one who didn't look suspiciously at him was loyal Judas Iscariot. Jesus then spoke quiet words to Judas and he left quickly. "Great," Simon had thought, "the only one who believes in me is gone now. I guess he took the money bag again to give an offering to the poor."

Suddenly, two feet stood inches from Simon's head, startling him from his thoughts. He rolled over to see Jesus towering over him. "Did I fall asleep again?" Simon thought. This time, Jesus did not call him Simon.

He did not have to.

The Carpenter's hands reached down to the hand of the fisherman and lifted him to his feet. The three didn't know what to say. The Rabbi had plenty to say, but He did not say a word. He returned again, praying the same words. "O My Father, if this cup cannot pass away from Me unless I drink it, Your will be done."

He would not close his eyes this time! He focused on the Lord, who was praying even more intently. Jesus seemed to have gone to a different place, but it wasn't a different place. But now there was something beside him, a rock? No, Jesus was in the same empty clearing, praying, but something was beside him. It moved! Simon gasped. It was not something, but someone! But whoever or whatever it was, it did not look human.

He glanced back to see if somehow James or John had gone down to pray with Him. No, they were behind him. Sleeping again? He turned back to see Jesus but now the Lord was all alone. Thick clouds had rolled in and maybe his eyes were playing tricks on him. Christ had been heaving, sobbing…almost writhing. It reminded him of the time he had seen Moses and Elijah on the mountain top. Only now did it dawn on Simon that he might have seen an angel from heaven.

As Simon watched, he thought he saw shadows shifting beneath the praying master, but the disciple soon discovered once again, he was wrong. Those were not shadows but puddles, dark drops of something pooled beneath Jesus's forehead as He prayed. Violently shaking, Jesus turned his head, eyes no longer looking heaven-ward, but clenched tightly shut. His Lord was not sweating but bleeding! Not from a wound but oozing from the agony of his prayer.

Simon tried coming closer, mesmerized as the drops plopped down again and again. Maybe he was shocked by the blood, but morbid fear fell upon the once calloused Simon. Time seemed to slow. He was more overwhelmed than when he had seen the naked, demonic man running towards them. He could not move. Sheer terror gripped his heart more strongly than when he was drowning in the middle of a night's storm raging on Galilee. Yet he was drowning but now in Gethsemane, but not with water. He could not stand. He fell down as if the clouds above had surrounded him, suffocating him out of consciousness. Exhaustion, darkness, wine, sorrow, accusing eyes, prophecies of failure, swirling of events, heated arguments with religious leaders, sleepless nights, cheering crowds, heavenly voices, swirled and swirled and swirled around his pounding heart.

"Get up," Jesus said commandingly, urgently. Peter jumped up in an instant, as did John and James. Confused, disoriented, Peter was not where he thought he had just been. Had he been sleeping yet again?

All of the disciples were now all surrounding Jesus. All disciples but one.

Judas Iscariot was approaching. With soldiers.

DAY 37: MORNING
"The High Priestly Prayer"
(John 17:1–26)

This chapter is truly the "Lord's Prayer" and is frequently called the "High Priestly Prayer." According to Hebrews, Jesus is the ultimate High Priest.

As the Son of God, He is always able to intercede for us. He is merciful and faithful as High Priest (Hebrews 2:17), who as the Son of God is more faithful and glorious than Moses (Hebrews 3:1–6).

As the Son of Man, He is a sympathetic High Priest, having been tempted in every way, but never sinned (Hebrews 4:14–15). God the Father glorified the Son in a priesthood greater than the Jewish practice through Aaron and the Levites (Hebrews 7). But this High Priest does not intercede for us on earth, in a temple, but rather in heaven in the very presence of the Father Himself (Hebrews 8:1–4). So great of a Priest is Christ that He only had to offer one sacrifice, once and for all, and now is seated at the right hand of the Heavenly Father (Hebrews 9:7–28).

Now that we see who this High Priest is, what does He pray for?

He prays for Himself (John 17:1–5)

He prays for His Disciples (John 17:6–19)

He prays for future Believers (John 17:20–26)

> **Hebrews 4:14-16**
>
> *We have a great High Priest, Jesus Christ the Son of God. He understands our weaknesses, because He was tempted just like we are, except He never sinned. But as a result, we can pray boldly and with power and know we will receive mercy and grace in our greatest times of need.*

Today's devotional had a lot of cross references to Hebrews. Ponder those verses carefully as you prepare to learn about prayer from our Great High Priest.

The following is a little different prayer than normal. It is a paraphrase of the Lord's Prayer or the Model Prayer. Pray it with the freshness of the wording given:

Pray this prayer to God: *"O Jesus, our Prophet, Priest, and King, teach me to pray even as You did with the disciples. Our Father in heaven, Your very name is sacred. Bring Your reign in my life as it is in heaven. Give me what I need today, and help me be content with You alone. Forgive our sins, and help us forgive those who have hurt us. Keep me from areas where I will sin, and rescue me from those evil things. Your kingdom is the entire universe. Your power is more than all of the powers of the cosmos combined. And Your glory, Your Glory, YOUR GLORY is forever and ever. Amen."*

DAY 37: EVENING
He Prays For Himself
(Read John 17:1–5)

The audacity of Jesus to pray for Himself! Is it selfish to pray for yourself? If so, why did Jesus pray for Himself and ask His Father to glorify the Son?

If you ride on an airliner and listen to the attendant talk about the cabin decompression, you may have wondered why they say to put the oxygen mask on yourself first and then put it on your child. Isn't that "me first" attitude toward providing life-sustaining oxygen a little selfish? Why would you put an oxygen mask on yourself first, before putting it on a child?

In Bruce Wilkinson's little but powerful book *The Prayer of Jabez,* the author imagines the Old Testament character praying to God with a seemingly selfish request:

In my mind's eye, I picture Jabez standing before a massive gate recessed into a sky-high wall…[R]aising his hands to Heaven, he cries out, "Father, oh, Father! Please bless me! And what I really mean is…bless me a lot!

Bruce Wilkinson, *The Prayer of Jabez*
(Sisters, Ore., Multnomah Publishers, Inc.), p. 22.

Similarly, Jesus prayed for God to glorify the Son, because when God does the glorifying, that glory is like light that is shot into a diamond—the brilliance of the glory is shown all around with even greater glory shone back onto the Father.

Jesus was the most selfless Being who ever existed, and yet He prayed for Himself. You also are commanded to "make your requests known to God" (Philippians 4:6).

In addition to His glory, Jesus prays about eternal life. Look at John 17:3 and see how Jesus defines "eternal life". Eternal life is not just going to heaven. It is having an intimate knowledge of God and Jesus Christ. J.I. Packer answered the question of "How can we turn our knowledge *about* God into knowledge *of* God?" this way:

The rule for (knowing God) is demanding but simple. It is that we turn each truth that we learn about God into matter for meditation *before* God, leading to prayer and praise *to* God…And it is as we enter more and more deeply into this experience of being humbled and exalted that our knowledge of God increases, and with it our peace, our strength, and our joy.

J. I. Packer, *Knowing God*
(Downers Grove, Ill., InterVarsity Press), p. 18–19.

Pray this prayer to God: *"Heavenly Father, I want to know You and Your Son Jesus Christ. Bring glory to me, that I might glorify You. Amen."*

DAY 38: MORNING
Jesus Prays For His Disciples
(Read John 17:6–19)

Possession (verses 6–10) In tenderly praying for them, Jesus declares God's "ownership" of the disciples. *"They were Yours, You gave them to Me."* As His possession, Jesus truly loved them and sought their very best. We too now belong to Christ. How valuable are we? Our purchase price was the death of God's only Son.

Protection (verses 11–12) Jesus prays for the protection of the disciples. Some versions say "keep"; others say "protect". The word is used again in verse 15 for God to protect the disciples from the evil one. Ephesians 4:30 says we are "sealed" by God's Holy Spirit.

Pleasure (verse 13) Jesus prayed for His joy to be fulfilled in them. God wants you to enjoy life here on earth. *"My joy is that your joy is full,"* (John 15:11). Jesus told a story about a man who sold everything to buy a piece of land (Matthew 13:44). The man, who represents Jesus, didn't mind the price. It was for "joy" that he sold everything for the hidden treasure. Heaven is called the *"joy of your Lord"* (Matthew 25:23). There is trouble in the world, John 16:33–34 says, but God gives us peace and joy. When you have joy, it is an answer to Jesus's prayer.

Purpose (verse 14–16, 18) We are in the world, but not of it. We are in the world for a reason. "I do not pray that You should take them out of the world, but that You should keep (protect) them from the evil one." For the disciples, and for us, there is a message to be carried to the world.

Purity (verse 17, 19) In verse 11, Jesus appeals to His Father as "Holy" which is the same word used for the "Holy Spirit" which is God's Spirit living in us. Holy means "sanctified," "consecrated," "set apart." That word is also used in verse 17 as "Sanctify them." The Bible repeatedly commands, "Be holy, for I am holy."

If you don't know who Pastor Tony Evans is, you need to go to **tonyevans.org** and listen to a few hundred sermons (more or less). Then imagine his voice explaining this:

"A Holy, Sanctified, Consecrated, Set Apart Father sets apart a set apart people who are kept with a set apart name, through the Set Apart Spirit by the Set Apart Son for a set apart life with a set apart purpose."

Think about what that means as you ponder God's purpose for you in this world.

Pray this prayer to God: *"As I pray to You, Father, I ask for what Your Son asked for the early disciples: Your ownership of my life, for You to keep me, for You to give me a purpose in this world, and to help me enjoy it. In Jesus's Holy Name I pray. Amen."*

DAY 38: EVENING
He Prays For Future Believers
(Read John 17:20–26)

Did you know that Jesus prayed for you? He did! Read it for yourself. *"I do not pray for these alone, but also for those who will believe in Me through their word."*

Did you see it? Write your name in your Bible at John 17:20, because that is where Jesus prayed for you.

Jesus prayed that you "all may be one," meaning for you to be one with others. Being one doesn't mean identical, but united. It's okay to be different, but it's not okay to be divided. Is there an individual that you are not "one" with? Is there a race or a social class against whom you are prejudiced? Is there a denomination or a worship style that is different than yours that you can't stand? Fulfill the prayer of Jesus and be at one with your fellow believers.

Jesus prayed for you to have His glory (verse 22). I don't know fully what it means to receive His glory, but one thing He makes pretty clear: His glory makes us one with others and with Him. If we aren't, we are keeping His glory from shining in us.

Jesus prayed for you to be a witness (verse 23). The best way to witness is through united love (verse 26). 1 John 4:19–21 says, *"We love Him because He first loved us. If someone says, "I love God," and hates his brother, he is a liar; for he who does not love his brother whom he has seen, how can he love God whom he has not seen? And this commandment we have from Him: that he who loves God must love his brother also."*

Don't just say you love others, show your love with your actions! Read 1 John 3:14–18: *"We know that we have passed from death to life, because we love the brethren. He who does not love his brother abides in death… And we also ought to lay down our lives for the brethren. But whoever has this world's goods, and sees his brother in need, and shuts up his heart from him, how does the love of God abide in him? My little children let us not love in word or in tongue, but in deed and in truth."*

Jesus appealed to God as "Father," "Holy Father," and "Righteous Father." Righteous means God will do what is right.

Jesus is still praying for you. Jesus *"is at the right hand of God and intercedes for us"* (Romans 8:34, HCSB). How awesome is His prayer for us.

Pray this prayer to God: *"Righteous Father. Make me righteous by faith. Help me to not only get along with others but truly be at one with them in love, so that I can be a witness to the world for You. I look forward to seeing You in glory and being with Your Son. Thank You, Jesus, for praying for me. Amen."*

—John Chapter 18—

MEMORY VERSE:
"For this cause I was born, and for this cause I have come into the world, that I should bear witness to the truth."

(John 18:37b)

Crushed For Our Iniquities

The Messiah had been here before, to the garden filled with orchards of olives. In fact, it was just the previous Sunday. That time, however, this man from Nazareth descended the rocky path from Bethany, only to be elevated by the chants of "Hosanna." This time, the Son of God climbed up to Gethsemane by way of Gehenna, a smoldering trash dump whose smoke undoubtedly stung the Lord's eyes and nostrils.

In years past, Gehenna had burned the flesh of boys and girls as apostate Hebrews offered their children to the false god of Molech. But it was not the smoke of rubbish or the memories of the stench of burned infants which brought tears to His eyes this night. It was the smoke of a far worse hell, a hell to where He soon would descend and from which His Father would raise Him up.

But He must retreat in prayer, in a place so serene, so peaceful. The place was called "The Pressing" or "The Crushing."

The Bible calls it, the Garden of Gethsemane.

DAY 39: MORNING
Submitting In The Garden of Agony
(Read John 18:1)

At the base of the Mount of Olives is a garden known as Gethsemane (Matthew 26:36; Mark 14:32), which is a Hebrew word meaning an oil press. How providential it is that Jesus agonized in prayer at the very place where olives were crushed down under such weight that oil was extracted.

Hebrews 5:7

Jesus prayed with "vehement cries and tears" and "was heard because of His godly fear."

God hears our prayers, and He answers according to His will.

The prayer of John 17 is before they cross the Kidron Brook. That prayer was the priestly prayer, but the one in Gethsemane as recorded in Matthew, Mark, and Luke was the prayer in which He surrendered to become the sacrificial lamb. That prayer time was sufficiently covered in other gospels and was not included in John's Gospel.

Luke 22:44 records that Jesus prayed with such intensity that His sweat dropped like great drops of blood, falling down to the ground. A web page classifies sweating drops of blood as "hematidrosis." The cause is great stress which ruptures the blood vessels around the sweat glands. The blood goes into the sweat glands and pushes the blood to the surface of the skin. (www.encyclopedia.thefreedictionary.com)

It was in a garden that mankind fell, and death began to reign (Genesis 2). It was in a garden that Jesus prayed for the cup of death to pass. It was in a garden tomb that Christ arose from the dead. The word "paradise" means a garden, and in paradise, we will be able to eat of the tree of life (Revelation 2:7).

Prior to Jerusalem's fall in AD 70, Titus destroyed all of the olive trees on the mount just east of Jerusalem, so the trees which are now in the Garden of Gethsemane cannot be traced to Jesus's day. However, the numerous trees that were there at the time would have provided protection had Jesus wanted to flee. In fact, all of the disciples were able to escape from the band of armed men and officers from the Jewish council.

The writer was certainly aware that the other gospels went into great detail of Jesus's prayer in Gethsemane, which might explain the absence in His gospel. Read the parallel accounts of Jesus's prayer in the garden, found in Matthew 26:36–46; Mark 14:32–42; and Luke 22:39–46.

Pray this prayer to God: *"Heavenly Father, I confess to You that my prayer life needs to be more passionate and even agonizing as Jesus's was. I also lay my requests before You, knowing that the greatest desire is that Your will and not mine be done. In Jesus's Name. Amen."*

DAY 39: EVENING
Strength In The Shadows of Betrayal
(Read John 18:2–11)

More than Jesus's prayer of agony, John was divinely inspired to recall the power of divinity that Jesus possessed during His arrest and trial. Jesus knew all things, including the fact that He was going to be betrayed by Judas. He may have even purposely planned to go to Gethsemane to avoid any disturbance at the house where they had just dined.

When the cohort came with weapons and torches, Jesus did not shrink back but boldly came forward, asking twice whom they sought. The reply of "Jesus the Nazarene" was a term of derision, since being from Nazareth was viewed with contempt. Jesus showed no sign of resistance but stated, "I AM" (the word "He" is not in the Greek text). The sheer power of His statement caused the mob to fall backwards to the ground.

It is at this point the other gospels record that Judas greeted Jesus with a kiss. Proverbs 27:6 says *"Better are wounds from a friend than kisses of an enemy."* In the darkness of the shadows of the olive trees, the only sure way the guards could grab Jesus was if Judas could quickly identify Him. The symbolisms of a close friend's betrayal with a kiss are poignant and prophetic. Psalm 41:9 foreshadowed the intimate betrayal, *"Even my own familiar friend in whom I trusted, who ate my bread, has lifted up his heel against me."*

Not only was Jesus unafraid, He showed His care for the disciples by asking that they be allowed to leave. Mark's gospel stated a young man fled naked, and Peter's resistance indicates the soldiers had every intention of taking the disciples as well.

Perhaps outraged by emotion over such an act of betrayal, Peter pulled out his sword and struck the servant of the High Priest. Luke 22:49 says Peter asked Jesus if he could strike but did not wait for an answer. I relate with Peter in that I often ask God what I should do after I've already decided. Other times, I try to "help God out" and base my actions on human abilities and reason rather than trust God. Like Peter, my emotions get the best of me, prompting me to ask God to forgive my rash actions.

Jesus firmly told Peter to put up His sword. Jesus did not need Peter's help. He was prepared to drink the cup that He had earlier prayed for His Father to take away.

As humans, we don't have the ability that Jesus had to foresee all things that are to come upon us (18:4). But Jesus knows the future, and we can ask His help to be prepared.

Pray this prayer to God: *"Dear God, I know that I don't face nearly the temptation to run away as the disciples faced. Help me to stand with You and follow Your guidance in my walk today. Remind me that You are in complete control and that I need to seek Your help, and not the other way around. Amen."*

DAY 40: MORNING
Sadness In Denying Christ
(Read John 18:15–18, 25–27)

John provides further light not covered by the other gospel writers. "The other disciple" in verse 15 is John, the author of the gospel. John was known to the priest and presumably to the girl who kept the gate. Surely a girl who knew John was a disciple should not have caused Peter to deny Christ...but she did!

Think about a situation in which you may have denied Christ, either verbally or with your actions. Now that the testing time has passed, should you have fallen?

It is interesting that John records Jesus as saying "Ego eimi" (I AM) when He was arrested and Peter declares "ouk eimi" (I am NOT, John 18:17 and 25) when questioned about being a disciple. We may deny Christ in word or deed, but Christ remains faithful to His mission. Paul would later write "when we are faithless, He remains faithful for He cannot deny Himself" (2 Timothy 2:13).

Peter's fear may have been because he cut off a man's ear. His criminal act of attempted murder, his rebuke by Christ, and his fear of being arrested all may have led to his three denials. In Peter's final denial, it was a relative of the servant who had actually been in the garden who confidently identified Peter.

The other gospels state that it was his Galilean twang that gave further evidence he was a disciple of Jesus. Like a child whose hand is caught in the cookie jar with crumbs all around his face, Peter stuck by his false story. Unlike a child, however, he uttered curses and swearing.

When convicted with sin, we need to confess our sins, seek restoration with those whom we have offended and forsake the sin. See Proverbs 28:13; Psalm 51:3; Daniel 9:20; Luke 15:18–22; 1 John 1:8–10; and Isaiah 1:18. The parable of the prodigal son and the later restoration of Peter in John 21 show that both God the Father and Christ are ready to restore our relationship, despite our failures.

Luke records that after his third denial, he and the Lord locked eyes with each other and that Peter left the court, weeping bitterly. We can run but we cannot hide from the conviction of our sins.

In our "denials of Christ," we will eventually lock eyes with Jesus. He will convict us, but with confession, He will also forgive us and restore us.

Pray this prayer to God: *"Lord Jesus, forgive me where I have failed You. I ask for strength to also forgive myself and forsake my sin. Help me not to give in to sin. In Your name I pray. Amen."*

DAY 40: EVENING
Standing In The Trials
(Read John 18:12–14, 19–24, 28–38)

Jesus was bound both to and from Annas's palace even though He offered no resistance. Jesus had eluded the officials before so they took no chances. Annas became high priest in AD 7. His son-in-law Caiaphas held the position, but Annas still held the power. John 18:19 and 22 refer to Annas as the high priest, (see Luke 3:2 and Acts 4:6).

The first of many blows Jesus was to receive came before Annas. Jesus answered questions in calm resolve throughout His trial. He refused to speak to Herod (Luke 23:9), who was responsible for John the Baptist's beheading.

God's ways are not our ways. It seems ironic that the same nation which had prayed for the coming of the Messiah would reject Him once He came. Aren't we the same? We pray for God's will, but when it comes, we reject it.

The chief priests and elders met to condemn Jesus to death and from there, Jesus was led to Pilate. John gives the greatest details about their interaction. By the time of John's writing, it is possible that guards or eyewitnesses in Pilate's own chamber had converted to Christianity to reveal these details undisclosed in the previous gospels.

All four gospels record Pilate asking Jesus whether He was the "King of the Jews," a title Pilate placed over Jesus at His crucifixion. When Christ returns, His name will be gloriously proclaimed as King of kings and Lord of lords (Revelation 17:14, 19:16). Oswald Chambers writes of Jesus's new name:

Our Lord returned to His original glory, but not simply as the Son of God—He returned to His Father as the Son of Man as well. There is now freedom of access for anyone straight to the very throne of God because of the ascension of the Son of Man. As the Son of Man, Jesus Christ deliberately limited His omnipotence, omnipresence, and omniscience. But now they are His in absolute, full power. As the Son of Man, Jesus Christ now has all the power at the throne of God. From His ascension forward He is the King of kings and Lord of lords.

Oswald Chambers, *My Utmost for His Highest*, May 17

Another irony is that even though He was innocent, Jesus was judged guilty before a godless throne, so that we though guilty could stand without judgment before God's throne. Because He stood faithful, we too should stand faithful in our trials.

Pray this prayer to God: *"Dear God, help me to stand in the trials of life. Strengthen me to face down whatever comes my way. Remind me that nothing will happen to me today that You and I cannot both handle together. Thank You for standing with me. Amen."*

—John Chapter 19—

MEMORY VERSE:
And he who has seen has testified, and his testimony is true; and he knows that he is telling the truth, so that you may believe.

(John 19:35)

I gave My back to those who struck Me, and My cheeks to those who plucked out the beard; I did not hide My face from shame and spitting. **Isaiah 50:6**

Just as many were astonished at you, so His visage was marred more than any man, And His form more than the sons of men. **Isaiah 52:14**

He is despised and rejected by men, a Man of sorrows and acquainted with grief… Surely He has borne our griefs and carried our sorrows; yet we esteemed Him stricken, smitten by God, and afflicted. But He was wounded for our transgressions, He was bruised for our iniquities; the chastisement for our peace was upon Him, and by His stripes we are healed. All we like sheep have gone astray; we have turned, every one, to his own way; and the Lord has laid on Him the iniquity of us all. He was oppressed and He was afflicted, yet He opened not His mouth; He was led as a lamb to the slaughter, and as a sheep before its shearers is silent, so He opened not His mouth…For He was cut off from the land of the living; for the transgressions of My people He was stricken. And they made His grave with the wicked--but with the rich at His death, because He had done no violence, nor was any deceit in His mouth. Yet it pleased the Lord to bruise Him; He has put Him to grief. When You make His soul an offering for sin, He shall see His seed, He shall prolong His days…For He shall bear their iniquities…He poured out His soul unto death, And He was numbered with the transgressors, And He bore the sin of many, And made intercession for the transgressors. **Isaiah 53:3–12**

DAY 41: MORNING
At The Trial
(Read John 18:28–19:16)

John's gospel shows the hypocrisy of the Jewish leaders, who would not go into the Praetorium so that they would not defile themselves for Passover. Look how many times Pilate had to go in and out of the Roman headquarters: Pilate went out (18:29), in (18:33), out (18:38), in (19:1), out (19:4), in (19:9), out (19:12) and apparently in and out once more for the conversation of 19:21 to take place, just to appease the Jews.

The fact that the religious leaders had met before sunrise (John 18:28 says it was early morning by the time they brought Jesus to Pilate), indicates they met illegally. They lied by saying Jesus was an evil doer and gathered false witnesses to convict him.

The leaders turned Jesus over to the Romans because they wanted Him crucified. Jesus knew the type of death He would die, as it had been prophesied in the Psalms and indicated in John 3 that He would be lifted up like Moses's serpent on the pole.

There is a profound explanation of why Jesus came. "For this cause I have come." What was that cause? To be sure, there were many reasons Jesus proclaimed in the gospels on why He came. But when Jesus was on trial, He made the "good confession before Pontius Pilate," quietly proclaiming why He came. *"For this cause I was born, and for this cause I have come into the world, that I should bear witness to the truth. Everyone who is of the truth hears My voice."*

While the religious leaders said one thing and did another, Jesus brought truth before the people. Jesus was the Truth in His life and in His witness of the Truth of God. Now we who are also of the Truth can hear Jesus and respond to Him.

Unfortunately, Pilate and so many in the world today hear the truth and then walk away, asking, "What is Truth?" Many today cannot handle the truth. Even more, they cannot live the truth without hypocrisy. Like the devil, they cannot stand in the truth (see John 8:44). John's perspective of the truth is crucial and in one of the smallest books of the New Testament, 3 John has the word truth or true seven times in 14 verses. *"I have no greater joy than to hear my children walk in the truth."*

Pledge yourself today to be as honest and true as you humanly can. The truth may hurt, but it also sets you free. Like Christ, be sure to join truth with grace (John 1:17), and like Paul's command, when you speak the truth, speak it in love (Ephesians 4:15).

Pray this prayer to God: *"Jesus, I confess You are the Way, the Truth, and the Life. Through Your Holy Spirit of truth, guide me in what is true. Help me to live in Your true word so that I can be set free indeed. Amen."*

DAY 41: EVENING
Are You The King Of The Jews?
(Read John 19:1–16)

It is likely between chapters 18 and 19 that Jesus was sent before King Herod. Three times Pilate declares, "I find no fault in Him" (John 18:38 with Luke 23:4, after being examined by Herod in 19:4 with Luke 23:14, and then finally in 19:6). With no help from Herod, except for the royal robe, Pilate has Him scourged, and the soldiers place on Him a crown of thorns, mocking His kingship.

Pilate's reluctance to crucify Jesus is stronger in John than in any of the gospels. Notice His questions, "Are You the King of the Jews? Am I a Jew? What have you done? Are You a King then? What is Truth? Where are You from? Are You not speaking to me? Do You not know that I have power to crucify You and power to release You? Shall I crucify your King?" Herod, a Jew, sought a sign, while Pilate, a Greek, sought wisdom. This point was made also by Paul in 1 Corinthians 1:22–25.

Salvation and knowledge of God does not come with a demonstration of a sign, and it doesn't come by having all of our questions answered. We come to know Christ by faith. Paul wrote, *"For Jews request a sign, and Greeks seek after wisdom; but we preach Christ crucified, to the Jews a stumbling block and to the Greeks foolishness, but to those who are called, both Jews and Greeks, Christ the power of God and the wisdom of God. Because the foolishness of God is wiser than men, and the weakness of God is stronger than men."*

As we learned on Day 36, you don't have to turn off your brain in order to become a Christian, and there are solid and good reasons to believe in God and Jesus Christ whom He sent. But wisdom and knowledge begin with a healthy fear and reverence for God (*"The fear of the Lord is the beginning of wisdom"* Psalm 111:10; Proverbs 9:10).

Seek God's answers from His Word, and then accept them humbly. Skeptics ask seemingly impossible questions only to justify their doubts and unbelief. Unlike Pilate and the Jewish officials, true seekers will find answers to their questions.

Pilate knew that the Jews had delivered Jesus up out of envy, and His sign above Christ's head as "King of the Jews" was to scorn the very people over which he ruled.

This devotional book has charted much territory over the past 41 days. We are about to reach the climax of this story. The question for you is: Is Jesus your King?

Pray this prayer to God: *"Lord Jesus, thank You for the stripes and beating You took for me. Give me Your truth and wisdom in my life, that I may show Your true Kingdom's rule in me. In the Holy name of Jesus I pray. Amen."*

DAY 42: MORNING
Pilate Did Not Bear The Greater Sin
(Read John 19:7–16)

When the Jews said Jesus *"claimed to be the Son of God,"* (NIV) Pilate became even more afraid. Perhaps something in his gut made him go back to the Man he had just flogged. Christ stood before Pontius Pilate wearing a mocking crown of thorns, His back scourged, His face marred. Still there was something unworldly about Him. "Where are you from?" Pilate asked, knowing He was a Nazarene. He meant something deeper, but Jesus gave him no solace for that nagging pit in his stomach. Jesus said nothing.

Had Jesus been a mere mortal man or not in such anguishing pain, He might have laughed scornfully at Pilate's feeble assertion that he had the power to release the Incarnate Liberator of those held captive and oppressed by sin (Luke 4:18). Surely Christ envisioned the twelve legions of angels tearing off the roof of the Praetorium and engulfing all His enemies with fire from heaven.

"Let me ease your guilt," the meek, bloodied Man seemed to be thinking about the man who was about to order Him to die. *"You could have no power unless it had been given to you from above. The one who delivered Me to you has the greater sin."*

The one? Possibly Jesus meant Caiaphas or even Judas, as more than 40 times in the New Testament the word *"delivered"* was translated as *"betrayed."* I know I am reading into this. I *know* Jesus did not have this in mind. But I am going to say it anyway. The one who delivered and betrayed Jesus, could it be … me? Could it be *you*?

There is no greater sin than *MY* sin. I can do nothing about YOUR sin. I can do nothing about the sins of Pilate or Judas or Caiaphas. But MY sin put Christ on the cross. It was for me He died. The one with greater sin than Pilate, who could have released him, Pontius Pilate, who scourged him, the one with greater sin could very well be ME.

I may not have put Christ on the cross, but His love for me put Him there and kept Him there. And Christ not only loves me that much, He loves you too.

I come away from today's reading wondering about Pontius Pilate, one who wanted to do one thing yet did the other, one whose internal conflict was won over by external forces. I see Pilate's failures mirror my own. I wonder "who has the greater sin?" Pilate, who had no idea who this man from Nazareth was and what the consequences would be. Or those of us who know Him as God's Son from heaven and by our actions, we too deliver and betray Him.

Pray this prayer to God: *"Thank You Father for hearing the prayers of Your Son, who prayed, 'lay not this sin against them, for they know not what they do,' even though we do know what we do. In Jesus's name. Amen."*

DAY 42: EVENING
The Compassion Of The Christ
(Read John 19:17–27)

Isaiah 53 says, *"It pleased the Lord to bruise Him."* God sent Himself in human flesh to die for us because He wanted us to have eternal life with Him.

Jesus's mother witnessed her Son's suffering. Others with Mary at the cross were her sister, as well as Mary the wife of Clopas, Mary Magdalene and of course John. Matthew and Mark record the mother of James and Joses (also named Mary), Salome and the wife of Zebedee, James and John's mother, were also there.

The Compassion of the Christ. Jesus was concerned for His mother. In His suffering, He cared for others, even for one of the thieves on the cross who had hurled insults at Him (Luke 23:43). Jesus also uttered a prayer for those who were crucifying Him. He heard the taunts of the rulers but didn't command the earth to swallow them up.

The compassion of the Christ was greater than that of any other human who has ever lived because it was not human love. It was the manifestation of God's incarnate love, exemplifying for us to look beyond humanity's short-fallings and sins, to live in a spirit of forgiveness, compassion, and love.

The greater the intimacy, the greater the capacity for being hurt, and with God's infinite love for us also came tremendous pain. Christ's pain was not only the physical suffering and mental anguish. The greatest pain of all came when Jesus took upon Himself all of the world's sins and absorbed and absolved them.

Many of you who read this have been hurt deeply by those whom you have loved richly. Perhaps you let your heart love freely, only to see that love rejected. Out of fear of ever being hurt like that again, you may have built up walls to keep you from love. This same John who watched his best Friend die, also saw his brother James killed for his faith. Ultimately, he outlived every other disciple who each died a violent martyr's death. Yet at the end of this martyr's life, John wrote these precious words: *There is no fear in love; but perfect love casts out fear, because fear involves torment. But he who fears has not been made perfect in love* (1 John 4:18).

That kind of love is not human love; it is perfect love. In a matter of days, Jesus will tell His disciples, *"As the Father sent me, so I send you."* Those tender words of compassion from a heart broken on the cross calls to you and me, *"Go and do likewise."*

Pray this prayer to God: *"Compassionate Father, I praise You for Your love for me. Help me see that the pain I feel does not come from the hatred in the world but from the love which Your compassion has placed in my heart. In the name of Jesus. Amen."*

DAY 43: MORNING
At The Death
(Read John 19:17–37)

Do you wish that your credit card bills would have stamped across it *Tetelestai?* Stamped what?

You would want that if you lived in the first century Grecian world. That word, *"Teh-TELL-es-tai,"* was actually a phrase used when bills are finally paid in full. *Tetelestai* signifies that Jesus finished all that He was called to do, and that our debt of sin is now atoned for. Jesus paid it all. Just before He died, He cried, *"It is finished."* "Tetelestai!"

It is finished. Jesus finished the work, and our sin debt is now paid in full. But without the resurrection, the crucifixion is not complete. Jesus had finished His work, and now the Father will do His work (1 Corinthians 6:14). Jesus earlier refused the numbing effect of vinegar-wine, but received it for His parched mouth so that He could utter His final words.

The Scriptures fulfilled. In the final hours, John notes the various Scriptures that were fulfilled, including many which Jesus had no control over, such as the dividing of His garments, His legs not being broken and His side being pierced. John gives the witness of fulfilled prophecy and also His own personal testimony that what He saw was true (19:35). See Psalms 22:18; 34:20; and Zechariah 12:10 for other prophecies.

There is power in the Word of God. Read John 15:3 *("You are already clean because of the word which I have spoken to you.")* and also Ephesians 5:26 *("that He might sanctify and cleanse her with the washing of water by the word")* The Scriptures have a cleansing power in our lives. Jesus fulfilled Scriptures from the Old Testament, so don't limit your reading solely to the New Testament.

Water and blood. From a medical viewpoint, we now know that those who die of a ruptured heart will have a sac of water membrane surrounding the heart. While Jesus gave up His spirit (verse 30, with *"Father, into Your hands I commit My spirit."* Luke 23:46), He died of a broken heart in a very real spiritual and physical sense. As a former disciple of John the Baptist, the writer saw the significance of the water as the cleansing power of repentance Jesus offered (Luke 3:3; 1 John 5:6). But that alone is not enough. The significance of the blood was the cleansing forgiveness of the Lamb of God (John 1:29; 1 John 1:7), which forever keeps us clean.

Pray this prayer to God: *"I glorify You, Jesus, for Your amazing grace and love that saved me. I praise You that Your atoning work is finished. Keep me clean by keeping me in Your word and in Your will. Amen."*

DAY 43: EVENING
At The Tomb
(Read John 19:38–42)

Matthew describes Joseph of Arimathea as rich, fulfilling the Isaiah 53:9 prophecy that Jesus would be buried in the tomb of a rich man. Mark states that with courage, he went boldly before Pilate to ask for the body of Jesus. Luke describes him as a good and just member of the Jewish Council who did not consent to the condemnation of Jesus. He and Nicodemus (see John 3; 7:50; and 19:39) were secret disciples but became bold in revealing their faith. The two hurriedly (and apparently not completely) prepared Jesus's body for burial.

The women who watched Joseph and Nicodemus felt the need to more completely prepare Jesus's body after the Sabbath day passed (Mark 16:1; Luke 23:56). The two men also rolled a large rock in front of the tomb, but Pilate was later requested by the Jewish officials to place guards around the tomb for three days. They also set a seal upon the tomb to prevent anyone from tampering with the stone.

Read Matthew 10:32–33: *"Therefore whoever confesses Me before men, him I will also confess before My Father who is in heaven. But whoever denies Me before men, him I will also deny before My Father who is in heaven."*

John explains that Jesus was crucified near a garden and buried in a new tomb in which no one had yet been laid. As a result of their actions, the two men would be ceremonially unclean for Passover, but their love for Christ compelled them to go before Pilate, purchase the burial materials, and openly profess their faith by their actions.

> **1 John 2:28**
>
> And now, little children, abide in Him, that when He appears, we may have confidence and not be ashamed before Him at His coming.

Think of a time in which you publicly professed your faith in Jesus Christ and think of what sacrifices you have made in continuing to have a testimony of being a Christian and a disciple. A disciple is one who disciplines his life to steadfastly follow Christ's teachings and example.

Commit to memory Romans 1:16 (NKJV):

For I am not ashamed of the gospel of Christ, for it is the power of God to salvation, for everyone who believes, for the Jew first and also for the Greek.

Pray this prayer of commitment to God: *"Dear God, I promise to You today to never be ashamed of Christ. I will profess Him openly to those I know and those I meet. Thank You, Jesus, for Your confession of me before our Father. In Your name. Amen."*

—John Chapter 20—

MEMORY VERSE:
So Jesus said to them again, "Peace to you!
As the Father has sent Me, I also send you."

(John 20:21)

John 20:21–22 are John's version of the Great Commission, or the authorization of the disciples (and all Christians) to tell others about Christ. Here is a listing of the other places where Jesus commissions us to tell others about Christ and His salvation:

THE GREAT COMMISSION IN THE GOSPELS:

[18]And Jesus came and spoke to them, saying, "All authority has been given to Me in heaven and on earth. [19]Go therefore and make disciples of all the nations, baptizing them in the name of the Father and of the Son and of the Holy Spirit, [20]teaching them to observe all things that I have commanded you; and lo, I am with you always, even to the end of the age." Amen.

Matthew 28:18–20

[15]And He said to them, "Go into all the world and preach the gospel to every creature. [16]He who believes and is baptized will be saved; but he who does not believe will be comdemned."

Mark 16:15–16

[46]Then He said to them, "Thus it is written, and thus it was necessary for the Christ to suffer and to rise from the dead the third day, [47]and that repentance and remission of sins should be preached in His name to all nations, beginning at Jerusalem.

Luke 24:46–47

[8]But you shall receive power when the Holy Spirit has come upon you; and you shall be witnesses to Me in Jerusalem, and in all Judea and Samaria, and to the end of the earth."

Acts 1:8

Faith Frees Us From Fear;
The Spirit Frees Us To Forgive

DAY 44: MORNING
Do You Believe?
(Read John 20:1–10)

All of the gospels record that Jesus arose on the first day of the week, or Sunday. More than 100,000 Sundays later, every week there has been some form of celebration of Jesus's resurrection. And it all began just before this sunrise recorded in John 20.

There are a number of reasons why we need to be in church and in fellowship with other believers. But there is only one reason why it is and has been on Sundays, especially Sunday mornings: **The resurrection!**

The law of resting on the Sabbath or the seventh day of the week was surpassed by a celebration of Jesus's proclamation of "It is finished." Sunday has become the Christian Day of Rest, setting apart Christ's triumph over death and the grave.

Although John only records Mary Magdalene as at the tomb, verse 2 and the other gospels show that there were indeed others with Mary. *"They have taken away the Lord out of the tomb, and **we** do not know where they have laid Him."*

Even with the evidence of the empty tomb and despite all of the prophecies of Jesus and the Scriptures (see Psalm 16:10) that He would rise again, Mary's first thought was that someone had taken His body.

Notice the urgency portrayed of Mary running from the tomb and Simon Peter and the other disciple, John, running to the tomb.

John lived into the mid-90s AD. He might have been in his teens or early 20s when Jesus died, since his parents are featured several times in the gospels. Peter was already married, so John's youthfulness likely aided him to arrive at the tomb first. Also, John's reflective nature and Peter's impulsiveness likely caused Peter to go into the tomb first.

I love the detail in the narrative here. John gives his eye-witness account of how he had to stoop down to look in. He also pointed out how the cloths were laid out, indicating that a grave-robber would not have left the linen and face cloths so orderly, certainly not with Roman guards outside the tomb.

When John followed Peter in and saw, something happened to John, according to verse 8. Peter went into the tomb and saw, but John went in, saw, and believed. The Bible doesn't say what John believed.

It doesn't have to say.

Pray this prayer to God: *"We praise You, Jesus, for Your resurrection from the dead. We confess our faith and belief in the Resurrection. Help me to trust in Your Word that what You have said, it will come to pass. In Jesus's Name, I pray. Amen."*

DAY 44: EVENING
Why Weepest Thou?
(Read John 20:11–17)

There is something so poignantly touching about this resurrection story, from Mary Magdalene's despair to Peter's exuberant race to the tomb and John's optimistic faith.

"But Mary stood outside by the tomb weeping." Those who have stood at a grave weeping know Mary Magdalene's heart. Her Master had delivered her from demonic possession (Mark 16:9). Mary had not lived a normal life. In today's world, we would say Mary "had issues." Mary undoubtedly loved Jesus deeply and He in a very holy sense also loved her. Tears blurred her vision. Sobs of mourning pierced the crisp spring air. She had seen the stone rolled away, but she again looked into an empty tomb for an answer to solace her question, "Where is He?"

Two angels in white now sat in the tomb. She didn't know or care who they were, as long as they could answer her confusion. King James beautifully poses their question, *"Woman, why weepest thou?"*

When you face grief, it is good to talk it out. God asks questions, but not to glean information but to let us verbalize what we are going through. Why would the angels and Jesus ask Mary, *"Why are you weeping?"*

The angels and Jesus knew why she wept. But in talking through grief, we can receive consolation. Pour out your heart to God. He cares. It was He who created our eyes to moisten when faced with grief or joy. Emotions are God-given and godly.

If you had seen Jesus's eyes as He watched Mary's despair, do you doubt that His own eyes would have been wet as well? Jesus loved Mary and like His Father and like the Holy Spirit, the Son also experienced emotions. Mary turned to Jesus but blinded by her tears and sorrow, she did not truly see Jesus. Only when Jesus called her name did she turn to Jesus in recognition. While there is godly sorrow, it should never eclipse our vision of seeing God and His purposes despite our sadness.

Mystery and myths have swirled around Mary Magdalene. Her response of "Rabboni" or "Teacher" hardly seems to validate such ridiculous fables which have been spread. If you hear any ridiculous fables that contradict the Bible, trust God's Word!

Newer translations of 20:17 convey the meaning of *"Touch me not"* (KJV). Mary was likely grabbing on to Jesus so tightly that He told her to *"stop clinging to Me."* He had not yet ascended to the Father and if He did not go, the Holy Spirit would not come.

Pray this prayer to God: *"Teacher, I give to You my tears. Teach me to cling to what is truly important. Teach me to find joy in what pleases You and to have sorrow over what grieves You. In Your name. Amen."*

DAY 45: MORNING
Seeing is Believing
(Read John 20:18–23)

When I was in high school, I knew a girl who, although quite young, had so much sorrow that she had built up walls of "protection" around her heart. Those walls which sheltered her from pain also imprisoned her from experiencing true trust, friendship, and God's love. I shared with her how Jesus walked through walls and locked doors, found in today's passage.

According to verse 19, the disciples were shut up in the room because of fear. When Jesus came through the shut doors, He announced the antidote to fear: His Peace.

One disciple who was apparently not afraid to be outside was Thomas, but it likely was not because he was at peace, which was Christ's antidote to fear. We are not told why Thomas was not present, but he had earlier expressed no fear of death when Jesus was going to Judea (John 11:16).

Later, Thomas expressed he did not believe and would not believe that Jesus was alive, no matter what the disciples said or claimed they saw. Ask yourself: What puts you into fear? What blocks doors for you? What makes you experience a lack of peace?

Know this: Jesus is the antidote to every answer you may have given.

The fear of the disciples was soon to be turned into joy. Mary Magdalene had told the disciples earlier in the day that she had seen the Lord. The other women had also seen Jesus along the road back to Jerusalem and, according to Matthew 28:9–10, His words to them were to give them joy and dispel their fears.

However, it was not enough for the disciples to hear of the experiences of others with the resurrected Savior. Each one of them, and each one of us, need to have that personal, liberating experience of Jesus breaking through the walls that bind us in fear. When Jesus appeared, He came into the room despite locked doors and walls of protective isolation. His first words were to unlock the doors and break down the walls with His peace.

John 20:21–22 are John's version of the Great Commission, or the authorization of the disciples (and all Christians) to tell others about Christ. Jesus wants you to personally experience the resurrection of Christ, and then share it with others.

Do you have walls built up that only Christ can break down? Are there doors locked out of fear of the world? Jesus will enter in and proclaim His peace. Let Him in.

Pray this prayer to God: *"Prince of Peace, I fall down at Your feet. Cast fear far from me and replace it with true inner peace and faith to testify of You and Your great salvation. Fill me with the fullness of Your forgiveness for others. Amen."*

DAY 45: EVENING
Not Seeing But Believing Is A Greater Blessing
(Read John 20:24–31)

While Thomas expressed no fear of death, he also apparently had no faith in Jesus's resurrection from the dead. Perhaps because Thomas was a twin, he knew what it was like to have a case of mistaken identity. The disciples may have simply been confused or saw what they wanted to see. Thomas, however, said he needed proof that they had seen the true Christ. Thomas is now renowned as "Doubting Thomas" but he is also a testimony that there is a need for a reasonable faith. Rather than condemning Thomas, Jesus appeared specifically to allow Thomas to examine the facts.

As Jews reckon days, "eight days later" was actually the following Sunday. Already the practice had begun of gathering the day after the Sabbath, or Saturday. This time, Thomas had no intentions of being left out of the gathering of the disciples. Jesus was very knowledgeable of what Thomas had said about putting his finger in the place of the nails and his hand into the side where the spear had pierced. The Bible doesn't say whether Thomas actually did either of those things once He actually saw the Lord.

Thomas's reply is a strong affirmation that Jesus is both Lord and God. Again, notice that Jesus does not rebuke Thomas for calling Him God, nor falling at His feet in worship. This is yet another reason that Christians believe that Christ is God in the flesh.

Chapter 20 concludes with a beautiful beatitude, a "blessed are those" statement. Blessed are those who have not seen but still believe is obviously speaking to everyone to whom John was writing and of course to all of us today.

Christ also affirms that those who have not seen Jesus and still believe are even more blessed. Except for the five hundred or so whom Paul refers to as seeing the resurrected Christ (1 Corinthians 15:6), all the rest of Christianity fall into the latter category of being blessed without seeing.

Finally, the purpose statement of John's gospel is found in verse 31. Fill in the blanks from the New King James Version:

But these are written that you may _____ that _____ is the _____, the Son of God, and that believing you may have _____ in His name.

Pray this prayer to God: *"My Lord and God, I believe and have faith in You. Take unbelief and cast it far from me. Replace my unbelief with faith and blessings. In the Holy Name of Jesus I pray. Amen."*

—John Chapter 21—

MEMORY VERSE:
*And there are also many other things that Jesus did, which
if they were written one by one, I suppose that even the world itself
could not contain the books that would be written. Amen.*

(John 21:25)

Epilogue to John's Gospel (John 21)

In John 20:30–31, the reader can sense a definite climax and conclusion to the gospel. It is the summation of the gospel, with Thomas's confession and profession of his faith in the risen Lord and God.

It appears that this final chapter was presented to explain the restoration of Simon Peter, and also explain John's long life. The other gospels were likely written prior to Peter's death. John, being a life-long companion to Peter, likely wanted to tell the story of Peter's restoration at Galilee (called "Tiberias" by the Romans).

Can you imagine being the Apostle John, writing down the final eyewitness gospel? He had seen his brother James killed. Then, Andrew, his best friend from his days with John the Baptist, martyred, crucified at his request on a cross in the shape of an X, unworthy to die like Christ. John outlived and had buried the precious Mary, the mother of Jesus whom His Lord entrusted to his care. He had read the biographies penned by Matthew, Mark, and Luke, pondered what they put in and, more importantly, what they left out.

He reflected on what others had written. He had preached many of these sermons at Ephesus. He saw fallacies and lies spreading about the Lord whom he had known personally. He had read and even received letters from Paul, then heard of his beheading in Rome, followed by Peter's crucifixion upside down in the same city. There had been too many deaths at the hands of his fellow Jews, only to be replaced by the Romans.

He was tired. He had journeyed to heaven during his exile to Patmos, written the book of Revelation, and he likely wished he could have stayed with his now white-haired, nail-scarred handed Lord in that heavenly realm. He had been boiled in oil, served as pastor of Ephesus, seen faithful followers fall away. It appeared that his cry of "Come quickly!" (Revelation 22:20) was not going to be answered by His Lord any time soon. So now what?

Many had undoubtedly asked John to transcribe his recollections of his short and now oh-so-distant three-and-a-half years he had spent with the Messiah. John truly reflected on the life of Christ and contemplated on the significances of Jesus's statements and miracles. His gospel would be fiery, yes, but deep and full of theology from the years of sermons he had preached. His young, tender heart had been prepared by John the Baptist and then he graduated to attend the best seminary in all of human history, taught by the Son of God and the Son of Man Himself.

But there is one more chapter to write…

DAY 46: MORNING
Look for Jesus
(Read John 21:1)

After the resurrection, the angels and Jesus told the women that Jesus would appear to the disciples at Galilee (see Matthew 28:7–8; Mark 16:7). Jesus appeared to two followers on the road to Emmaus (Luke 24:13–32), to Simon Peter (Luke 24:34) and in Jerusalem Sunday evening after the Resurrection. At some point, the disciples went to Galilee.

Jesus had said to remain in Jerusalem in Luke 24:49, but there appears to be a gap between Luke 24:43 and 44. The same writer, Luke, explained in Acts 1:3–4 that Jesus appeared to them several times over 40 days. John 21:1 says that *"Jesus showed Himself <u>again</u> to the disciples at the Sea of Tiberias,"* indicating that the first appearance to Thomas in John 20:26 could have been in Galilee.

1 Corinthians 15:5–7 says, *"⁵and that He was seen by Cephas, then by the twelve. ⁶After that He was seen by over five hundred brethren at once, of whom the greater part remain to the present, but some have fallen asleep. ⁷After that He was seen by James, then by all the apostles."* Most of Jesus's followers were in Galilee. "All the apostles" likely means those who had been "apostled" or "sent out" in Luke 10:1. *"After these things the Lord appointed seventy others also, and <u>sent them</u> two by two … where He Himself was about to go."*

Although the Bible never tells us specifically, He surely appeared to His own mother, Mary, and the rest of His brothers, who are next seen in Jerusalem with the 120 disciples in Acts 1:14 after Jesus ascended to heaven.

Jesus went to Galilee because it was there He had been so well received and where people would have been anxious to see Him alive. John 21 is the third appearance of Jesus to the disciples, but not the last time Jesus would appear. Read Hebrews 9:28 about how Jesus will appear to those who look for Him: *"Christ… will appear a second time for salvation…to those who eagerly await Him."* Hebrews 11:6 says, *"He is a rewarder of those who diligently seek Him."* James wrote, *"Draw near to God and He will draw near to you."* (James 4:8).

If you want to see the Lord spiritually, you must seek Him and He will come to you.

Pray this prayer to God: *"Father, I want to draw nearer to You and to have You come nearer to me. Reveal Yourself to me today as I seek You. Thank You for rewarding those who seek You. Amen."*

DAY 46: EVENING
Fishermen Or Fishers Of Men?
(Read John 21:2–11)

You can take the fishermen out of the sea, but you can't take the sea out of the fishermen! Seven men went out on the boat and after an all-night expedition, they caught nothing. The two unnamed disciples may have been Andrew and Philip.

In John 1:41, Andrew told his brother and fellow fisherman Simon about Christ. In John 1:45, Philip brought Nathanael to Jesus. If the two unnamed disciples in chapter 21 were in fact the first two "evangelists" in chapter 1, it may be a humble reminder that *we* never save anyone, but merely lead others to the Savior.

We may do the catching but God does the cleaning!

The disciples may have wondered, "Now what?" Jesus told them to go to Galilee. Jesus appeared to them there, this time with Thomas present, as He promised. And now? Fishing was more than a hobby for Peter. It was an income. There is a sense of aimlessness in this part of the story, especially for Peter.

Once you come to Christ, there is no going back. Even if you fail as Peter did, Jesus will restore you. If you try to live your life like you did before you met Christ, you will not only come up empty-handed, but empty-hearted. With Christ, your net will be filled to the fullest.

When given a choice between a boat-load of fish or Jesus, Peter left the fish, jumped into the lake to get to Christ! As he swam, I wonder if he thought about his attempt to walk on water (Matthew 14:29). Did he recall Jesus's first call for him to be a fisher of men rather than a fisherman (Mark 1:17)? Surely, he recalled his first miraculous catch of fish (Luke 5:5). As he emerged soaking wet, Peter saw the fish and bread on the fire. Did he recall the five loaves and two fish (John 6:9)? Did he remember how the wind and the seas obeyed Christ in the storm (Matthew 8:27), and wonder if the fish simply came ashore at the Lord's command?

One more memory may have come to Peter and he dried and warmed his hands around a coal fire. But before we look there, here is a question for you: Are you looking for Jesus, but not living for Jesus? If you seek an encounter with God, are you prepared to give an accounting to Him, as Peter soon would do? That is confession. God will forgive you, but you must forsake your old ways of life.

Pray this prayer to God: *"Like Peter, I sometimes want to pray 'Depart from me, Lord, for I am a sinner.' Once again I confess my failures. And once again, I seek forgiveness. Fill my net with the only thing that can truly satisfy—Your presence in me. In Jesus's Name. Amen."*

DAY 47: MORNING
How Do You Soften A Rock?
(Read John 21:12–18)

Forgiveness.

It is hard to forgive others. But oh, to forgive yourself, now *that* is a task.

This passage is about Peter's three-fold restoration at Galilee. This morning and this evening we look at three questions, three responses, and three commands. On this third visit, Jesus asked Simon three similar but slightly different ways, "Do you love Me?"

Peter had so many good qualities, but also so many faults. The Bible says as soon as they came ashore, they saw a charcoal fire. The only other time this word is used in the Bible was when John and Peter warmed themselves at a charcoal fire in front of the High Priest's courtyard (John 18:18) when Peter denied Christ three times. Perhaps the fire reminded Peter that while Jesus had forgiven Peter, Peter had not forgiven Peter.

Notice what Jesus calls Peter…Simon, son of Jonah. When Jesus first met Simon, He changed his name to Cephas, or Peter, a stone or a rock. Later, Jesus reiterated Simon bar-Jonah's name change in Matthew 16:17–18 when Peter professed Jesus to be the Christ, the Son of God.

But now Jesus called His disciple "Simon, son of Jonah." Simon was one of the most common names in the New Testament, there were two Simons among the twelve apostles, one of the brothers of Jesus was named Simon, there's Simon the Leper, Simon the Cyrenian, Simon the Pharisee, Simon the father of Judas Iscariot, Simon the Sorcerer, Simon the Tanner, not to mention all the Simeons, which is the Hebrew form of Simon. Simon son of Jonah was a common, regular man.

The Lord, now resurrected, knew all things. He knew at this Galilean breakfast that in less than 40 days, Peter, the Rock, will preach one of the most powerful sermons in all of Christian history at the very place where Simon, the Regular, had been terrorized by a servant girl on the night Jesus was on trial. Jesus knows Peter's potential. Peter does not. Jesus will reveal it.

Has Simon learned his lesson? Will the Rock soften his self-reliance and solidly rely on Christ? Talk was cheap the night before Simon, the Regular, denied Christ three times. Peter, the Rock, will be tested and restored so that he soon can walk the costly walk.

Pray this prayer: *"Lord, You know all things. If You want to know how much I love You, You know not to trust my words, but my actions will show. I will show You my love for You in showing it to those whom You love. Thank You for meeting me where I am and loving me anyway. Amen."*

DAY 47: EVENING
Do You Love Me?
(John 21:12–18)

"Simon, son of Jonah, do you…" and here we must learn some Greek. The word "love" here is *agape* pronounced "ah-gah-PAY" or "uh-GAH-pay" (definitely not "uh-GAPE" as it is pronounced in English). It is the highest, most selfless type of love. *"Do you love (agape) Me more than these?"* Our Lord surely was referring to the other disciples and not to fishing (although some avid fishermen may need to answer that!).

Peter remembered his brash bragging that if all else left Jesus, good ole Pete would be there for Him. *"Yes, Lord, you know I…"* and here Peter responded with a word for love that is softer than *agape* love. It is *phileo*, pronounced "fil-LAY-oh." It is a friendship love, stronger than "liking" someone but we could use that here. "Yes, Lord, You know that I strongly like You." Peter did not say he loved Jesus more than the other disciples. Peter responded without bravado or overstating. Jesus said, *"Feed My lambs."* Peter likely returned to looking at the fire.

The Lord is not nearly done. *"Simon, son of Jonah, do you <u>agape</u> love Me?"* Peter had no idea where Jesus was going with this. This second time, Jesus lessened his question slightly, not saying *"more than these"* but "do you love Me, still with *agape*, love with abandonment, with no expectations, just pure godly love?"

Unprepared to answer more astutely, Peter responded identically with the *phileo* love. *"Yes, Lord, You know that I 'strongly like' You."* Jesus replied with a similar but different command, *"Tend my sheep."*

Do you feel Peter's awkward, uncomfortable feelings? If he had a collar, he would be pulling on it, clearing his throat, wishing he could be anywhere else than under Jesus's unflinching gaze. A third time it came. *"Simon, son of Jonah, do you…"* wait for it… *"love (<u>phileo</u>) Me?"* Maybe the inflection was "Do you *even* 'strongly like' Me?

Ouch! *"Grieved was Peter…"* The Greek puts "grieved" at the first of the sentence to emphasize Peter's emotional response. Grief flooded back like the sobs he heaved after the rooster crowed. *"Lord, you know all things. You know…"* long pause. What will he say? *Phileo? Agape?* Has humility taken hold of his heart? Will he succumb to proud but empty promises? *"You know I <u>phileo</u> love You."* Jesus responds with a slightly different third command, *"Feed My sheep."*

Ponder Jesus's question as if He were probing you with His searching eyes and searing question: "Do YOU love Me?"

Pray this prayer to God: *"Lord, You know all things. You know that I love You. Probe me as You did Peter, not to grieve me, but to restore me. Amen."*

Day 48: Morning
From Remorse To Restoration
(Read John 21:12–19)

When we fall, it is important not only to admit our mistakes and abandon our wicked ways: we must make amends. Peter was sorry (remorse) for his denials. He would never make that mistake again (repentance). But for full restoration, there must be more than remorse and repentance--there must be restitution. Restitution means doing something to make amends for what was taken. It is not a punishment but it benefits the victim and the perpetrator. Jesus restored Peter by giving him something to do.

"Feed My lambs" (John 21:15) or those who are young in the faith. Peter would soon be the first "elder" of the young church. An elder does not mean the oldest man in the church, but rather someone who is spiritually mature. To feed lambs means to gently nourish and lead them to maturity.

Secondly, Jesus charged Peter to *"shepherd My sheep"* (John 21:16, HCSB). This emphasizes the pastor's role of protecting of the more mature flock of God. One of the favorite analogies Jesus used was calling His people "sheep," so naturally he also referred to Himself as a Shepherd (John 10:11,14; Mark 14:27). He gave Peter one of the highest compliments in calling him "pastor" or shepherd.

Jesus restored Peter by calling him to *"feed"* (the same word in verse 15) the mature church. Peter was to be an overseer of the flock, young and old. The serious charge was followed by a prophecy that Peter's commitment would lead to death.

Jesus then restored Peter by calling him to "follow Me." All pastors are to follow the Chief Shepherd as leaders of the flock. Peter would later give that same charge to young pastors coming after him. See 1 Peter 5:1–5 (NIV):

[1]To the elders among you, I appeal as a fellow <u>elder</u>, a witness of Christ's sufferings and one who also will share in the glory to be revealed: [2]Be <u>shepherds</u> of God's flock that is under your care, serving as <u>overseers</u>--not because you must, but because you are willing, as God wants you to be; not greedy for money, but eager to serve; [3]not lording it over those entrusted to you, but being examples to the flock. [4]And when the Chief Shepherd appears, you will receive the crown of glory that will never fade away. [5]Young men, in the same way be submissive to those who are older. All of you, clothe yourselves with humility toward one another, because, "God opposes the proud but gives grace to the humble."

Pray this prayer to our Good Shepherd: *"Jesus, Lover of my soul, thank You for not only forgiving me, leading me to repentance, but also for restoring my life to You. Set me apart, so that I can restore others when they fall. Amen."*

DAY 48: EVENING
Will You Follow, No Matter The Cost?
(Read John 21:17–19)

Just as this study is drawing to a close, Jesus's ministry was winding down and only a few more lessons for the disciples to learn in the presence of Christ. After every profession of Peter's love, Jesus responded with a command to action. "Tenderly feed the young believers. Shepherd the mature believers. Feed the mature believers" (my paraphrase). True love calls us to action.

In John 10:5, Jesus had taught all of the disciples and especially Peter about how sheep follow the shepherd because they know his voice. *"they will by no means follow a stranger, but will flee from him, for they do not know the voice of strangers."* Peter knew his Master's voice and although he soon would no longer audibly hear it, he would follow His Chief Shepherd until the day of his death.

On that horrible night, only hours before his three denials, Jesus said, *"Where I go, you cannot **follow**, but later, you will **follow** Me."* Peter said, *"Lord, why can't I **follow** You? I will lay down my life for You!"* (John 13:36–37 NIV, emphasis mine).

Following Christ is costly. The call to follow is not limited to a few and neither is it without sacrifice. Peter's walk with Christ began with a call to follow and it ends with a call to follow. Dietrich Bonhoeffer died a martyr's death at the hands of Adolf Hitler only days before Germany's liberation. He knew the cost of following and wrote years before his death in the book *The Cost of Discipleship* (pages 44–45):

"When Christ calls a man, he bids him come and die."
"Such grace is costly because it calls us to follow…
…and it is grace because it calls us to follow Jesus Christ.
It is costly because it costs a man his life…
and it is grace because it gives a man the only true life.
It is costly because it condemns sin…
…and it is grace because it justifies the sinner.
Above all, it is costly because it cost God the life of his Son: "ye were bought at a price," and what has cost God much cannot be cheap for us…
…Above all, it is grace because God did not reckon his Son too dear a price to pay for our life, but delivered him up for us.
Costly grace is the Incarnation of God."

Pray this prayer to God: *"Lord, lead me this day to follow You. Help me count the cost of following You so that I can share in the grace of following You. Amen."*

DAY 49: MORNING
What Is That To You? You Follow Me
(Read John 21:20–23)

Something happens when Jesus calls us to follow Him. Suddenly our focus will go somewhere else -- anywhere else -- than where Jesus is calling us to follow. You have gone through nearly one hundred devotionals in the gospel of John. It is up to you on whether you will follow Christ. Prepare to get distracted from following Christ.

From the shores of Galilee, Peter had followed Christ, leaving his nets and boat to become a fisher of men. He had followed Christ to a mountain to see Moses and Elijah and Jesus transfigured. He had followed the Lord to see a dead girl raised. He heard Jesus call people to follow. Some obeyed. Others did not. Peter professed that *"we left all and followed You,"* (Luke 18:28) when nearly everyone else had stopped following. He had followed Christ so closely, he even walked on water, and then so distantly that he even denied Christ with an oath. Even now, Peter did not fully understand what it meant to "take up his cross" and follow Christ. Peter turns from literally following Jesus to see John "also following."

Why did Peter ask about John? There may have been some jealousy...John reclined with Jesus at the final supper. The *"disciple whom Jesus loved"* had an inside connection with Jesus that made John's mother ask for John and James to sit at Jesus's right and left hands. Jesus had even called John to take care of His own mother Mary.

Jesus responded by focusing Peter's gaze back to the path of following Christ. Perhaps as you follow Christ, your focus may drift to others rather than to Christ. Let His words to Peter fill your mind and your heart, *"What is that to you? You follow Me."*

Jesus looked to the future and the end of Peter's life. It is as though Jesus said, "You can't go back to your old self-centered ways. And where you're going will be difficult. But even in death, you will glorify Me. Now follow Me."

John sensed his own death approaching and had heard the rumors that he just might live until Jesus returned. He wanted to set the story straight. Jesus did not say John would live until He returned but that it was really no one else's business! The point Jesus was making was, "It doesn't matter how Jesus deals with other people. That is His business! You need to follow God!"

Pray this prayer to God: *"God, take any and all distractions away from my focus as I seek to follow You. Thank You that You have gone before me and have prepared the path in which I am to walk. Amen.*

DAY 49: EVENING
I Suppose ...
(Read John 21:24–25)

Do you *suppose* that John could have *supposed* what has gone on for the last two thousand years? Could he have *supposed* all that has been written about this Carpenter from Galilee? Go to a Christian book store and see that truth of John's final statement *"I suppose that even the world itself could not contain the books that would be written."* We still have not finished writing about this Jesus of Nazareth!

Perhaps John actually finished his gospel in chapter 20 and then as age approached him, he wanted to quell the theory that he would live until the Lord returned. Maybe he was (like I am) reluctant to close this study. John knew that many had already written about Jesus and more would still be written.

It's not just books that have been written about Christ. The first film ever made about the life of Christ was released in 1902 (updated in 1905 and now it has even been colorized). I have lost track on how many films and television dramas have been made about Jesus. It appears the world may not be able to contain **the books** about Christ but also **the films** about Jesus.

I hope you have watched the 2003 film, *The Gospel of John.* Another film, the *Jesus* film (1979), is the most translated film in history and also the most viewed movie of all time. *The Passion of the Christ* (2004) is financially one of the highest grossing films of all time (in excess of $370 million at the time of this writing).

None conveys all of what Jesus did. Then again, neither does John's gospel. John left parts out. John put in enough that you would believe that Jesus was the Christ, the Son of God, and that you would receive eternal life. None would write--could write--as John did. He had been there. Peter wrote in his epistle, *"We did not follow cunningly devised fables when we made known to you the power and the coming of our Lord Jesus Christ, but we were eyewitnesses of His majesty,"* (2 Peter 1:16).

John was likely the last eyewitness and he along with Andrew had been the first eyewitnesses, before Matthew, Mark and Luke; before Peter and Paul, before any of the other disciples. All of the eyewitnesses Luke had consulted (see Luke 1:2) were now gone. John knew this was the last gospel, the last chapter, the last word.

But is it? By no means! We continue the story of Christ. I suppose (rather **I know!**) that there are still more chapters to be written. Go write the next chapter in the ongoing story of Christ!

Pray this prayer to God: *"As I finish this study, keep me following You. You know that I love You. Lead me to feed others. In Your Great Name of Jesus I pray. Amen."*

About the Author

Timothy C. McKeown is a minister serving at First Baptist Church in Killeen, Texas. He began his call into ministry in 1984 as a youth pastor in Parker County, Texas, and began writing devotionals on John when he could not find a good devotional for new believers on this foundational gospel. While he was a bi-vocational pastor for a number of years, Timothy also worked as a journalist and editor for several Texas newspapers. He went into full-time Christian ministry in Brownsville, Texas. He has since served in Tyler, Whitehouse, and now Killeen. He and his high school sweetheart, Melissa, have two sons, two daughters-in-law, two daughters, a son-in-law, two grandsons and a granddaughter, and a kind dog named Rocky.

Visit him online at www.timothymckeown.blogspot.com.